THIS BOOK
BELONGS TO:-

David Winter.

CHAMPAGNE

CHAMPAGNE

Henry McNulty

Collins,
8 Grafton Street, London W1X 3LA

First published in 1987 by
William Collins Sons & Co Ltd
London · Glasgow · Sydney
Auckland · Toronto · Johannesburg

First impression 1987
© 1987 The Paul Press Limited

British Library Cataloguing in Publication Data
  McNulty, Henry
  Champagne
  1. Champagne (Wine)
  I. Title
  641.2'2 TP555

  ISBN 0 00 412326 3

Typeset by AKM Associates (UK) Ltd., Ajmal House,
Hayes Road, Southall, London UB2 5NG
Originated and printed in Singapore through Print Buyers' Database

This book was edited, designed and produced by
The Paul Press Ltd, 41-42 Berners Street, London W1P 3AA

Project editor EMMA WARLOW
Art editor CLAIRE GILCHRIST
Cover photograph DON WOOD
Cartography CHRIS MOORE
Index JILL FORD
Art Director STEPHEN McCURDY
Editorial Director JEREMY HARWOOD

Contents

Introduction

Since time immemorial, Champagne has been associated with pleasure, luxury, sensuality, and intensity of life. Without question there is something unique about the wine that is as much charged with love, invention and care as it is with bubbles.

The French believe that Champagne is no mere earth-bound wine, but a symbol of the soul and spirit of mankind. It is the wine of carnival, of humour and of gaiety, and it certainly lifts its drinkers' spirits up into the stratosphere. One little glass makes a very fine aperitif, which serves above all to increase your anticipation of the next. Two or three glasses bring with them gaiety and euphoria. It is surprising what a good proposition Champagne is for an evening's drinking, since there is no threat of suffering "the morning after" – as long as you don't mix it! Wine lovers over the years have united in praise of its many virtues. The eminent economist, Maynard Keynes, is said to have remarked that his only regret in his life was that he had not drunk enough Champagne.

Champagne is indispensable at celebrations because it is an inherently happy wine. It always seems to strike the right note, making any special event more exciting, eventful and entertaining. Champagne is drunk to launch new business enterprises or to celebrate promotion; a roughly handled bottle, spouting like a fountain, is an integral part of the winning scene after a major Grand Prix championship; a bottle (sometimes embarrassingly difficult to break) is smashed over the bows of a ship at its launch; and the wine is almost a necessity at a wedding party. The extent of its appeal across the world is only equalled by the variety of ways in which it is enjoyed.

There can be no hard and fast rules about how Champagne should be drunk, because it is such a very personal wine. The French were very tolerant of idiosyncratic drinking habits when it comes to Champagne and indulge in several themselves. The officially accepted way to open a bottle is quietly, with a sigh rather than a bang, but unofficially the Champenois say: "The more popping the better!" A Champenois friend of mine has told me that putting ice in Champagne is anathema – "like using butter with cheese". But I have seen another equally traditional Champenois put ice cubes in his Champagne glass on a hot summer day, saying with a wink: "Don't tell anyone."

The greater the variety of tastes, the better, as far as the health of the Champagne industry is concerned. Some people prefer to drink their Champagne from flutes, others from tulip glasses or *coupes*. Some prefer their wine extra dry; others like it sweet. Some like it young; others like it mature. People drink Champagne at all times of the day and night, at parties or in solitiude. *Rosé* Champagne is many people's favourite kind, while others dismiss it as a fad. All preferences are equally valid.

Champagne may be synonymous with all that is fine in life, but it is not just a symbol. It is recognized as one of the world's best wines, on a par with a great Bordeaux, or a Burgundy. It should be enjoyed as a fine wine, as well as something to be drunk on special occasions. Making fine Champagne is not a matter of luck; it requires intuition, dedication and years of concentrated experience.

Probably the most important thing to remember about Champagne is that it is a blended wine. The more old wines a firm carries in its cellars, the greater the range of sources it is able to tap when making its blends. A wide choice of wines to blend also helps a firm to keep the style and quality of its wines consistent, year after year. A non-vintage wine can often be superior to a vintage, because its blending is not restricted to the wines of a single vintage year. Such a wine will have a balanced blend that a vintage wine made from a single crop will not be able to achieve. A non-vintage is also more likely to improve with age because of this carefully adjusted balance, whereas a vintage wine is intended to be drunk comparatively young. Vintages, of course, have their own redeeming features, such as a special flavour and aroma that can come only from using the best grapes in a particularly successful year.

The blending of wines to produce the perfect individual style of Champagne is perhaps the most crucial element in the whole production process. The reputation of a firm relies on the skill of its *chef de cave* or blender. This skill is derived from years of intimate knowledge of the Champagne vineyards, their grape varieties and other qualities. Quite a number of well-known Houses own no vineyards at all, and have established their names with wines made from the highest quality grapes, bought from the best growing areas. The *chef de cave* supervises the selection that suits his personal formula and instigates the blending process.

The care and precision involved in the creation of Champagne results in a wine with a truly "spiritual" quality. Nature provides the ingredients, but Man is there at every step of the process to bring out the best in them. For classic breeding, Champagne has few rivals in the wine world, and in what follows I hope to demonstrate how its exclusive reputation was born and is maintained today. Champagne is not just an irresistible wine; it has a timeless mystique and once you fall for its charms you will never look back.

Henry McNulty

Champagne: The Region

"*L*a Champagne", the geographical country of Champagne, is where "*Le* Champagne", the wine, is made. The name is a rather imprecise one, since the area of Champagne no longer exists as a political entity as it did during the Middle Ages. Medieval Champagne covered more or less what are now the three modern French *départements* of Marne, Aube and Haute Maine. Champagne vines, as an agricultural entity, are today officially only grown in certain parts of the Marne, the Aube and the Aisne. Of these *départements*, by far the most important for wine production is the Marne, which includes Champagne wine's most prestigious production centres. Reims and Epernay are the twin "capitals" of the vine, with vineyards in the sub-areas of the Montagne de Reims, the Vallée de la Marne, and the Côte des Blancs.

The regimented lines of the grapevines at Villedommange, crystallized in a coat of frost on a winter's morning. The produce of this *premier cru* village is made into some of the finest wines of Champagne.

The region is blessed with the essentials for growing Champagne vines: good soil, a subsoil of chalk and a wonderful range of mini-climates. It forms part of the "Parisian Basin", a geological depression that was once the bed of a huge sea. The vineyards are concentrated around Reims and Epernay, but are generally dotted over the whole region, growing wherever the soil suits them, and wherever an area conforms to the official regulations controlling the right to call the wines produced there "Champagne".

The whole area is well supplied with rivers. Northwest from Reims, for about 25km (15mi) along a little river called the Vesle, is a small dependency of vineland villages. To the south, vineyards line the valleys of other streams – the Aube, the Ardre, the Surmelin, and even the upper reaches of the Seine. In the east, the limit of vineyard lands is a rolling plain spreading as far as the foothills of the Vosges mountains, known to the ironical local population as la Champagne pouilleuse (or "flea-bitten"), presumably because the region lacks the distinction of the more wooded, well watered, hilly areas of the other parts of the Champagne countryside.

To the west of Epernay, the vineyards stretch for about 125km (75mi) along the Marne Valley into the Brie country (where Champagne's famous cheese is made), finally petering out just before reaching Meaux, 67km (40mi) from Paris. To the south there are even vines on the banks of the infant Seine and along the Aube, at Bar-sur-Seine and Bar-sur-Aube.

A rigorous climate
All this flowing water helps to keep the climate of Champagne on a fairly even keel. Strangely enough, Champagne's unreliable sunshine and non-uniform temperatures contribute to the quality of its wines, because the rigours of the climate force the vines to overcompensate. The discerning imbiber gains, because the wines are more interesting. "The climate of the Marne gives the grapes a *finesse* and lightness that forms the principal merit of their wines", according to Dr. Jules Guyot, a famed specialist in wines and vines in the mid-19th century. The vines of Champagne are claimed to be able to produce about twice as much juice from their grapes as their more sun-kissed relatives in the south of France.

The whole region lies relatively far north for wine growing. In fact, the Champagne vineyards are the most northern of any of the important vineyards of Europe apart from a few that struggle against the climates of northern Germany, and some small ones in the UK. The reason for the continued success of the wine industry, against the seasonal odds, is that Champagne is the lucky possessor of several mini-climates, each with its own variations of grape type, and its own blend of soils.

Annual variation, too – cold winters, warm summers – is of great importance to Champagne wines. The hills provide three kinds of mini-climate, of which the favourable ones are the suntraps formed in the folds of slopes. There are plenty of unfavourable pockets, however, where frost, fog, rain and hail are the principal worries. The river valleys help to rationalise these good and bad elements, and make for more equable, constant weather conditions. Most importantly, Champagne's rainfall is comparatively steady all the year round, averaging 177 days of rain a year.

The Champagne Vineyards
One of the most important and prestigious parts of the officially recognized vinelands is the Montagne de Reims, whose vineyards occupy the northern slopes of the Montagne (a plateau only 300m (328yd) high that lies between Reims and Epernay). The vineyards occupy every nook and cranny of the "mountain's" folds, following along the northern slopes from the hamlet of Chamery, directly south of Reims, to the village of Trepail, to the east, where the Montagne curves down and around in a huge horseshoe to the southern slopes of the same mountain. Here the vineyards change name, being known as the vineyards of the Vallée de la Marne.

The vineyard villages of the Montagne de Reims include Rilly, Sillery, Verzenay (where stands Champagne's one and only aggressively individual windmill), Verzy, Villers-Marmery, Billy (pronounced Bee-yee), and Trépail.

Between the northern and southern slopes of the Montagne de Reims, a plateau harbours a dense forest, which is full of game – fallow deer, pheasant and boar –

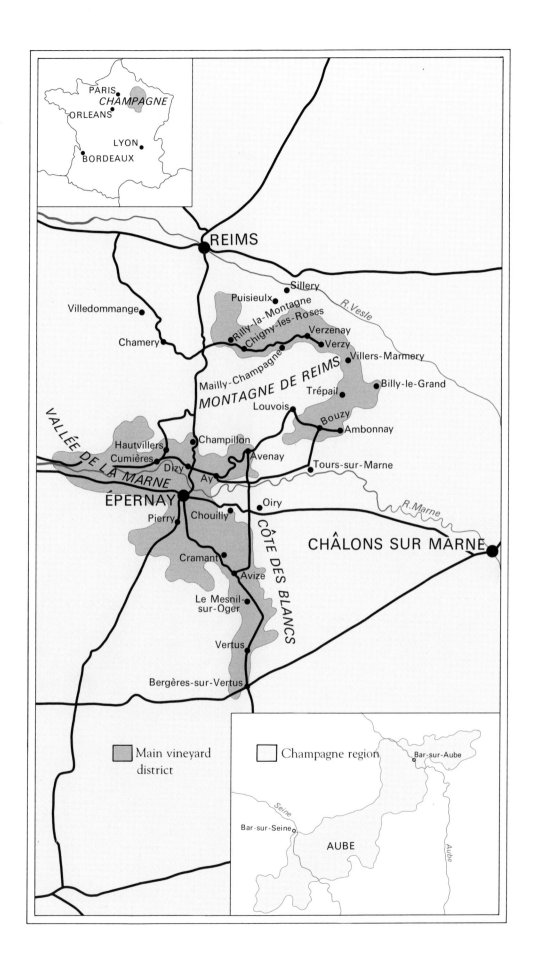

despite the persistent attacks of the local *vignerons* and *citoyens* during the open seasons. Out of season the forest is a favourite site for walks and picnics. Just before entering the forest from Epernay, there is an unencumbered and magnificent view of the vineyards below, which stretch to the horizon.

The village next to Trepail on the horseshoe, Ambonnay, is the first of those in the Vallée de la Marne vineyard region, though it is still on the slopes of the Montagne. The village next to Ambonnay rejoices in the perhaps significant name of Bouzy (known for its still red wines, as well as its sparkling ones); then come Louvois, Avenay, Ay (just across the Marne from Epernay, but still on the Montagne) Dizy and Hautvillers.

The vines stretch westward from Epernay in clumps, on both sides of the Marne, becoming less and less productive as they pass Château Thierry and approach Paris at Dormans, about 100km (60mi) from the capital. The prestige of their wines is not as high as those of the villages that I have already mentioned.

The third of the prestige regions, the Côte des Blancs, lies to the south of the Marne, just beyond Epernay and again south from there to Vertus. A series of little villages includes Pierry, Cramant, Avize and Le Mesnil. Even farther south, there are more small islands of Champagne vineyards on flatter land around Sézanne, spreading intermittently in patches to Bar-sur-Aube; and below Bar-sur-Seine, in an area called Bar Séquanais.

Champagne vines are also found at Colombey-les-deux-Eglises, about 30km (20mi) south of Bar-Sur-Aube. Colombey, the former home of General Charles de Gaulle, is one of the famed Medieval market and fair towns that helped to make Champagne prosperous before the local population discovered how to make sparkling wine of excellence.

The lie of the land

The Montagne de Reims may not be imposing as a mountain range, being more like a large bump between the rivers Vesle and Marne, but it produces Champagne's best grapes. On the Vesle lies Reims itself, one of the twin centres of the Champagne industry for over 100 years. On the Marne,

across the Montagne de Reims, to the south, is Champagne's second city, Epernay. Reims takes the lead, perhaps, on the commercial and marketing side, Epernay on the administrative and production side. But both are almost equally important to the success and maintenance of the prestige of Champagne.

Traffic on the main road over the Montagne de Reims between Reims and Epernay is constant. So is work in the vineyards. Shops and streets are full of what

seem to be happy, busy people. There is a general air of well-being in the land. In between the towns and spreading far to the east and west lies Champagne's secret underground ingredient; its very special subsoil of chalk, left behind by the sea that once covered nearly all of France. This chalk is largely composed of the fossil remains of billions of ancient shellfish that existed in the Tertiary Period of Geology, some 60 million years ago. The chalk subsoil fans out in a big bow curving around the

The prestigious vineyards of the beautiful village of Cumières, which nestles by the banks of the Marne on the southern slopes of the Montagne de Reims, belong to and supply some of the most famous Champagne Houses.

Hundreds of tourists visit the region every year, attracted by its delightful towns and villages where they can sample the wines of Champagne. Official "routes" guide them along the more scenic paths.

Montagne de Reims, bulging eastwards towards the Vosges mountains, gradually becoming more hilly as it nears the Franco-German border.

As you travel around the area you may come across places where the road has been sliced through topsoil and subsoil, showing clearly how the topsoil, from only about 45cm (18in) to a maximum of 2.7m (9ft) thick, forms a covering for the chalk subsoil, which at times reaches downward some 183m (600ft). Chalk makes an ideal sort of "petrified humus" for growing grapes. It holds moisture in reserve, like a natural cistern, so that the thirsty vine roots, pushing their way through this crumbly rock, can depend on a supply of water even in dry times.

Reims is now connected to Paris by a direct autoroute, the A4 super highway that rolls on to Strasbourg, passing through

the centre of the city. It lies some 142km (85mi) from Paris, about an hour-and-a-half's drive at the French speed of *deux cent à l'heure*. The autoroute passes through some lovely, rolling countryside, but the adjacent landscape has been so manicured that you get no impression of being in an interesting countryside. There is not a single grapevine to be seen! You feel that you might just as well have stayed at home. But if you are not in a hurry the old route, following more or less the course of the Marne river, is more interesting.

From Paris the N3 passes first through Meaux, a typical medieval country town, whose sights include a fine old cathedral and ancient ramparts. Shortly after Meaux, the Champagne vineyards being to appear as the road makes its way to Château Thierry, scene of some of the bloodiest encounters of the First World War, and birthplace of the famed teller of fables, Jean de la Fontaine, whose 16th century home can be visited. Outside the city, at Belleau Wood, a huge military cemetery commemorates the second battle of the Marne where thousands of "doughboys" gave their lives to help drive the Germans out during five weeks of the summer of 1918. Still following the picturesque, tree-lined course of the Marne, you reach Dormans, a small country town where the road splits and you may either go to Epernay by the right fork of the N3, or to Reims by the RD 380 to the left. On the way to Epernay, the road winds through vine-covered hillsides and charming wine-producing villages, eventually arriving in a bustling, small, French country town whose main avenue, the Avenue de Champagne, displays the impressive offices of half of the most prestigious names in the Champagne world, including those of the biggest producer, Moët & Chandon. Beneath the town run miles of cellars, criss-crossing under warehouses, offices and shipping platforms. These are not ancient like the *crayères* of Reims, but were built during the 18th and early 19th centuries.

Epernay was badly damaged during the First World War. So there is little of historic interest in its buildings. It is however of great significance in the Champagne world, both because some of the greatest Champagne Houses are based in the town, and because it is the seat of

the *Comité Interprofessionnel du Vin de Champagne*, the organization that coordinates the regulations of the government with the practical needs of the vintners and marketing experts in the Champagne industry.

The branch of the road to Reims is somewhat flatter, but at its end you reach a more modern city whose buildings are mainly new, and whose suburbs have largely sprung up since the Second World War. During his Presidency, De Gaulle thought to make Reims a kind of satellite city of Paris, capable of housing some two million people. The project was started, but although much was built, the buildings remained only half filled until just recently. Now the new town looms on Reims' horizon like a miniature New York, complete with wide boulevards and super-highways passing through it.

The magic of old Reims

The old town holds the other half of the prestigious Champagne names and some of the most historically and architecturally interesting buildings in France. Like most places in the Champagne area it has suffered tremendous battle damage over the centuries, but especially so during the bombardments of the two World Wars.

The town of Reims suffered horrific damage during the First World War as a result of the bombardment by the notorious long range cannon, "Big Bertha". Its cathedral has been extensively and meticulously restored.

There are extraordinary things to see, nevertheless: among them the impressive 13th century Reims Cathedral, and the Gallo-Roman Champagne cellars cut from the clay subsoil.

Reims is probably the only city in the world that has actually named one of its streets "Rue Rockefeller". This is because the cathedral was given a huge grant for its restoration after the First World War, by J. D. Rockefeller himself. Photographs taken in 1918 show the utter destruction caused by the indiscriminate bombardment the city and the cathedral suffered from the infamous long range cannon, "Big Bertha". Today, thanks largely to Rockefeller money, the cathedral has a new roof and the restoration of its interior and its population of remarkable statuary is still going on. The completed restoration work is extremely well done. Today it is hard to believe that this great cathedral was a burnt-out shell after the War, and the whole edifice is again well worth seeing. One of the most charming pieces in the cathedral is the marvellously happy figure of a robed angel to the left of the main portal. Known as the "Smiling Angel" the figure seems to be looking rather more than beatifically at what one can only guess might have been an empty glass of Champagne in its right hand. (No glass is there, but what else could produce such an enchanting smile?) Inside the cathedral there is a superb modern stained glass window, designed by Marc Chagall, that was donated by the Champagne *négociants* and *vignerons*.

Next door to the cathedral are two museums. In one, the Musée Tau, some of the original statues that fell from the façade during the bombardment are shown at nearly eye level. Gigantic in size, the sculptures are both interesting and very moving. The other is the Musée St. Denis, where some wonderful paintings by Cranach, Corot, David, Renoir, Picasso and others are on show. The most interesting of its exhibits, in my opinion, is a series of 10 painted cloth hangings, showing scenes from the life of St. Denis in minute Medieval detail.

Reims was used for 600 years as the place for the coronation (*sacre*) of the Kings of France – there were 27 in all, beginning with Louis VIII and ending with Charles X in 1824. Records exist of some of the food that was provided by the local authorities for the Royal entourage during the *sacre* of Philippe VI of Valois in May of 1364. In spite of war and hard times, they feasted on 82 head of cattle, 85 calves, 289 sheep, 78 pigs, 345 bitterns and herons, 2000 young geese, 800 rabbits, 18,000 chickens, 492 pates of eel, 4000 crayfish, 40,000 eggs, 200 carp, 700 pike, 250 salmon, and a few barrels of sturgeon, for good measure.

The famous crayères

Apart from the outstanding cathedral, the most impressive of the sights on offer at Reims are the Champagne cellars themselves, dug out of the white chalk of the city's underpinnings. These are truly remarkable: startlingly white, hand-chiselled walls soar upwards from some 30m (100ft) below the surface to the world above, in inverted pyramids. The original excavation dates from Roman times. The Romans began to use the chalk for building – for although it is so soft when underground and away from the air that you can scratch "graffiti" on it with a fingernail, once it is brought to the surface and exposed to oxygen it hardens rapidly into stone. In fact most of old Reims, including the cathedral, was built from this material.

In order to prevent premature exposure to the air while the chalk was being cut, the Romans started by making an opening at the surface, small enough so that it could be covered by a trap door when not in use. From this opening the stone was cut outwards and downwards to form a hollow pyramid with a base that often covered some 30m^2 (320ft^2) – sometimes in the form of a square, sometimes in a rather irregular oval or circle. The French call these pits *crayères*. They make ideal cellars for Champagne and have often made ideal hideaways for the local population in times of trouble above ground.

The quarries were abandoned when the Romans were driven out of the area by the Huns but even then they were used as hiding places by the natives to avoid being slaughtered by the Hun. The early Christians, too, are said to have used them to avoid persecution in much the same way as the Christians of Turkey hid from Moslem fury in the canyons of Urgup in the Anatolian plateau. Certainly during the religious wars between Catholics and Protestants in the 16th century, the first converts to Protestantism used them clandestinely to prevent the Catholic authorities from disturbing their services. More recently, during the First World War and in the last war, the cellars did duty as bomb shelters. Part of the population lived in them as semi-permanent homes – pictures show citizens happily dining at trestle tables underground in what seems almost total domestic comfort, while above them "Big Bertha" bashed away at their real homes and their cathedral.

The white chalk walls of Champagne's unique *crayères* have been decorated in many instances with beautiful sculpture. The most prolific of the *crayères* artists were the Navelets, who executed this bas relief for the House of Mercier.

The perfect cellars

Nowadays the *crayères* serve a rather less exciting purpose. From about 6m (20ft) below the surface to as far down as they have been dug, the temperature in the *crayères* is a constant 10–12°C (50–54°F) all year round – perfect for storing wine. The chalk absorbs any moisture or condensation so the cellars are not at all humid. In some of them a harmless fungus – related to penicillin – forms. Many years before Sir Alexander Fleming discovered pencillin's healing properties, ancient cellarers used the fungus as a kind of unguent when they got small cuts or abrasions at work!

Because of the way they were excavated – from a small opening, spreading out to spacious floors below – the bases of adjoining cellars were often found to be close to each other. It was then a simple matter to pierce connecting passageways between *crayères*, thus creating a network of underground rooms.

It took a long time for the Champagne houses to realise that they had such perfect ready-made wine cellars. The first to use them for this purpose was Claude Ruinart in 1769, but his competitors did not take advantage of the ideal storage space until the middle of the next century. Today, tens of millions of bottles of champagne are piled up in the cellars, peacefully ageing. The piles are turned constantly as the old bottles become sufficiently mature to be disgorged, labelled and shipped to the world's markets.

Some of the *crayères* have been turned into veritable palaces for entertaining visitors and prospective customers. At Ruinart the old Roman entrance holes have been glazed in, so that the *crayères* are partly lit from above. The walls of four *crayères* at Pommery have been sculpted into huge white tableaux, arranged as a bas-relief art show to represent different festive occasions over the years when Champagne has been drunk. In them, too, is a very large cask, capable of holding 75,000l (16,700gal) of wine, which was carved for the St. Louis Exposition of 1904. A new, fifth, tableaux has just been carved to mark the 100th anniversary of Madame Pommery's death.

So far some 250 of these Gallo-Roman cellars have been found in the area. Champagne bottles need plenty of space, however – 100,000 bottles require about 200m² (2153ft²) for storage – so not all

The staff of Pommery & Greno at the turn of the century, standing proudly on the steps leading down to the *caves*.

of Champagne's stocks of maturing wine can be kept in these ancient cellars. There are many miles of more recently quarried cellars in both Reims and Epernay – especially in Epernay, where there are no Gallo-Roman ones. Even the Champagne cellars that are not *crayères* are impressive. Moët and Chandon, together with Mercier and Ruinart which they now own, have a total of 24km (15mi) of them. Piper Heidsieck has a private electric train to take visitors around its 16km (10mi) of bottle piles. Pol Roger had a landslide in 1900 that brought down several floors of its caves and wrecked over a million bottles stored in them. They were rebuilt, and all is now well. The total underground mileage of all these storage cellars comes to a 400km (250mi).

The People

The Champenois, as the natives of these winelands are called, are a mixture of peoples, having lived in a hotbed of war and commerce for centuries. They are a combination of smart, industrious farm workers and owners (*les vignerons*), who produce and sell their grapes to an equally smart and industrious set of their colleagues in the wine trade: sophisticated businessmen, international merchants, salesmen, blenders, shippers and aristocrats (*les négociants*). All Champagne people are prodigious workers, and not at all the *bon vivant* types you might expect in a world that makes its living from the most effervescent of products, the very soul of gaiety and happiness. They are talkative, thrifty and full of commonsense, but, although they tend to be reserved, they have an artless sense of humour. I have always found that the Champenois are among the friendliest people in the world.

But the face of Champagne is forever changing. Since the Second World War, the mixture of its inhabitants has become even more complicated. No longer is the population almost wholly devoted to the vine. It supports computer experts, manufacturers of automobile parts, and the dozens of other trades that today compose any fairly large cosmopolitan area. Many Champenois are direct descendants of noblemen and courtiers of the Medieval courts of the Counts of Champagne, and nowadays belong to the modern élite of the international jet set and the international business world.

It is difficult to define the true origins of the "native" Champenois. An expert could probably detect traces of Roman blood; Spanish eyes left over from the days when Spain ruled the nearby Low Countries; and strains of the Celt who came from the Atlantic regions of France, possibly accounting for the poetic way in which they speak and write. There are even Asiatic-looking Champenois; descendants of the Huns who invaded Champagne around 2500 years ago. As the historian Hippolyte Taine put it, the Champenois "is a product of his race, his environment and the moment" – in short anyone who lives in the area becomes an adopted Champenois.

The Champenois can be as cheerful as anyone else when things seem to be going well in the vineyards. At the little town of Essoyes, in the Aube, for example, there was a Champagne fair recently. The attractions included: a gigantic fountain in the shape of a Champagne bottle as its centrepiece; the coronation of a "Queen of Champagne"; initiations into the "*Commanderie de Saute-Bouchon Champenois*" (in free translation, "The Order of the Cork-Poppers of Champagne"); 15 floats; bands from all over Europe, including the pipe and drum band of the US Nato forces in Europe; and a souvenir glass of Champagne for everyone.

Essoyes is the village where Auguste Renoir worked for more than 20 years. He bought a house, and a vineyard, where he could work "without being bothered by the *vignerons*, who had other things to do than to decide the future of painting". His opinion of the Champenois was high. As he wrote to his agent, Vollard, "I have excellent butter here, and bread like nothing you can find in Paris – and then, this 'little *vin du pays*' " and added that he liked being among the Champagne wine growers "because they are so generous".

The towns of Champagne

Near the centre of Champagne's wide, bulging belt of chalk subsoil lies Châlons-sur-Marne, which was once a bustling commercial city, influential in the Champagne wine industry.

In the 19th century, Napoleon III built a huge military training centre in Châlons, which is still an important unit in France's army organization. The handsome, pure Gothic cathedral of St. Etienne was used for the royal weddings of Louis XIV's brother, the Prince of Orléans, and that of the Grand Dauphin, in the 17th century. Now largely an industrial town, Châlons' wine trade has been taken over by Reims. But it is still important to Champagne because it is the seat of the Prefecture of the Marne. The Prefect is in charge of the activities and proper functioning of the CIVC, the organization that supervises the maintenance of Champagne's quality, sets its grape prices, and polices its operations in general.

In the Middle Ages, Châlons was the principal city of Champagne, so declared by Henri III because it took his part in the wars against the Austrian empire. "Hardly an officer or good bourgeois of Châlons does not have his own vineyard", one contemporary wrote. These vintners kept what wine they needed for their own households, and sold the rest to Reims or Paris. Châlons was the home of Frère Oudart, a priest who was a contemporary of Dom Pérignon.

He is credited with being one of the first to use *liqueur de tirage*, that helps to bring on Champagne's second fermentation. An important figure in the history of the wines, Frerè Oudart was cellar master at the abbey of St. Pierre-aux-Monts, and ably managed its vineyard estates at Pierry, Cramant and Chouilly.

Châlons still plays a vital role in the success of Champagne, however: enormous nurseries nurture the vine grafts for Champagne's vineyards. European grape varieties are grafted on to American roots: these are immune to the phylloxera plant louse, and are thereby protected from this destructive pest.

Another important city of Champagne, its old quarter nestling in a curve of the river Seine, is Troyes. Once a thriving cultural and commerical centre, the old part of the town is filled with picturesque narrow streets, and half-timbered, overhanging Medieval houses. It was formerly the region's capital, and home of the powerful Counts of Champagne, who made Troyes the site of their renowned international Fairs. Held twice a year these ran for 49 days, bringing together merchants from Flanders, Germany, Italy and all over France, to buy and sell spices, dyes, wool, leather, and to enjoy the local wines. They helped to turn Champagne into a prosperous centre of commerce, and left another legacy in Troyes' museums, which are full of fine ancient art, updated today with some wonderful Impressionist and Fauvist paintings.

In the 12th century, Count Henri I founded 13 churches and 13 hospitals in the city. He also sponsored the Fairs, but his nephew, Count Thibaut IV, made them famous. Thibaut was a very cunning businessman, but he was also a poet, and he made Champagne into a centre of French literary and cultural life.

In 1420, Isabel of Bavaria signed a "wretched treaty" with the English, whereby she disinherited the Dauphin and agreed to the marriage between her daughter, Catherine of France, and Henry V of England. As a result, the English and the Burgundians became masters of Troyes, and remained so until Joan of Arc won the city back in 1429.

A place of history
The Champagne region, having been a battle ground for centuries, no longer has any true "ethnic" personality. Not only has it been ravaged by all kinds of invaders, but it has also been a commercial crossroads. Even in the Middle Ages it was very cosmopolitan. Visitors came through it (and some of them stayed on in business), from Germany, England, the Netherlands, Portugal and Spain, Italy, and Provence and Savoy (then still states in their own right). Surprisingly, however, despite all the destruction and mayhem of the last two World Wars, the countryside is lovely, dotted with interesting villages and towns, many of them full of Romanesque churches.

Standing lonely in the countryside are a number of menhirs (single standing stones) and dolmens (rough, prehistoric buildings made with several huge flat stones) left behind by prehistoric builders, no doubt to puzzle and amaze us. And there are remains of huge Roman military camps, like the one at St. Erme, to show the enormous efforts that were made to keep the barbarians at bay.

By an astonishing quirk of nature, five of France's major rivers start in the Plateau de Langres on the southern edge of the Champagne region – the Seine, the Marne, the Aisne, the Meuse and the Aube. The Seine splits off to the East almost immediately and finally flows through Paris to the sea at Le Havre, but the others meander through Champagne, often connected to each other by canals. There is even one canal that allows barge traffic to sail directly into the Rhine. The Aube springs out of a spectacular cave about 5km (3mi) south of Langres. The mouth of this cave is closed by an iron grill, while above it on the hilltop is "Fort Vercingetorix", commemorating one of Caesar's respected opponents some 50 years before Christ. The Meuse starts less dramatically from the Plateau de Langres, and flows by Joan of Arc's birthplace at Domremy, 15km (9½mi) from Bar-le-Duc and the frontiers of Champagne, then on into Belgium.

Champagne: The Tradition

The Champagne country is used to being invaded, though its inhabitants have probably never enjoyed the experience overmuch. For centuries before Caesar wrote about the area in his "*Gallic Wars*", dozens of roaming, marauding barbarian bands had fought each other for parts of its territory. These wild tribes were mainly Gauls who finally established themselves in the northwest corner of what is now France.

The breathtaking façade of Reims Cathedral, which has been restored to almost pristine condition since its devastation in the First World War thanks to generous donations.

The Romans in Champagne

The Romans arrived to save the local Gauls (and their own conquests) from being overrun by even wilder Teutoni and Cimbri from the east. They landed in southern Gaul (now known as Provence) in 121BC. Between 57 and 52BC, the Romans thrust north, conquering the formidable opposition of the Gallic chieftain, Vercingetorix, en route. Reims (the capital of the local tribe, the Remes) became a federated city of the Roman Empire and was given the unwieldy name of Durocortorum. The ancient Roman city gate, the Porte de Mars, battered as it has been by successive wars, is all that is left of the former Roman wall of the town. It still stands on Reims' outer boulevards as witness to the city's importance nearly 2000 years ago.

From Caesar's day the Romans governed Gaul for almost 500 years by means of a series of treaties with the natives. It is generally believed that it was the civilizing and protective influence of the Roman Empire that marked the beginning of a flourishing Champenois wine industry. Previously, wines of any sort had been a luxury and in early Roman times they were mainly imported from Italy. Before the invasion of the Romans, the Gauls had drunk a kind of barley wine, and it is unlikely that there were any vines in the Champagne region. There is evidence, however, that vines were being cultivated by the end of the fourth century AD, during a period of unprecedented peace.

This interval of calm, and indeed the Romans' hold over the country, was rudely shaken when savagely fierce tribes to the east, led by Attila the Hun, began to invade Roman Gaul from across the Rhine. Some bloody fighting ensued in the Champagne region, with the Romans and their allies initially taking the upper hand, pushing the Roman frontier eastwards into what is now Germany. In 406AD, however, the Vandals, with the Huns and the Franks again breathing hotly down their necks, crossed the Rhine and chased the Almani tribe into Alsace, while the Franks moved into the Champagne country. By this time Christianity had obtained a strong foothold. One of the barbarians' first pleasantries was to decapitate St. Nicaise on the porch of his earliest cathedral of Reims. (The city had

welcomed its original bishop – St. Sixte – in about 290AD.)

The Romans fought hard, but their power was definitely weakening under the waves of barbarian assault and the decline of their Empire. This was despite the assistance of the local monks, whose *spitting* power was apparently fairly devastating. Saint Alpin of Châlons caused such a deluge by spitting at Attila from the city ramparts that the Hun invader was terrified into retreating: St. Loup had a similar success at Troyes when he caused a thick fog so confusing to Attila that, once again, he was forced to retire.

Clovis, king of the barbarian Franks who invaded Champagne towards the end of the fifth century AD. He was converted to Christianity by St. Remi, when the miraculous powers of the young Bishop of Reims helped him in his wars, and he eventually became King of France.

Attila the Hun and his barbarian warriors at the battle of Châlons, where the Romans, led by Aetius, succeeded in driving him out of Champagne. Attila's legendary cruelty struck fear into the hearts of his enemies, but he could not resist the superior might displayed by the Roman forces in this conflict.

But it would have been most uncharacteristic if the Romans had departed without a final burst of glory. The Roman General Aetius, combining with the Visigoths of southwestern France, finally forced Attila to leave. He fought a decisive and victorious battle on the Catalaunian plain of the Champagne country, which was probably somewhere between today's Epernay and Châlons-sur-Marne, in the year 451AD.

Civilizing the barbarians
Among the earliest reliable evidence we have that wine was being drunk in the Champagne region is a legend concerning Saint Remi, the 22-year-old Bishop of Reims who was intent on converting the barbarians of Champagne to Christianity. At the end of the fifth century, Louis Clovis, an unconverted chieftain who led the tribe that was seeking supreme power in France, begged Bishop Remi for spiritual help in his attempt to drive his enemies from Champagne. Clovis promised Bishop Remi that he would convert to Christianity if he won a victory.

St. Remi sent Clovis off with a keg of local wine that he had blessed, telling him that Clovis and his army would be able to fight and win for as long as the wine lasted. Clovis and his warriors drank what they needed, but while they were fighting, try as they might, they never managed to drain the cask. When Clovis had finally conquered the enemy and returned to his Reims headquarters to report his triumph, the cask promptly ran dry. Clovis kept his promise, was baptized, and later was crowned King of France in Reims by his benefactor.

Bishop Remi seems to have made a habit of arranging miracles when it came to wine. Another legend tells of the embarrassment of the hosts when the wine ran out, rather early in the proceedings, at a celebration held to mark a "virgin's consecration of God". The Bishop found a single keg in the house that contained a few dregs of wine, fell on his knees and "prayed fervently". Immediately, the keg filled with wine, overflowing so that it splashed on to the paving stones. Thereupon, the virgin gave all her property to St. Remi's church.

Despite his conversion, Clovis did not become squeamish. He disposed of several rivals by a series of assassinations, thereby easing his way to total control over the throne of France. (When he died, in 511, he left a stable kingdom which his descendants – the Merovingian Dynasty – ruled for some 200 years.) However, his conversion did allow the monks a fair degree of freedom from persecution. This gave them time to develop their role as innovators of much that was best about Medieval life. They improved the lands near their monasteries; they built roads, dammed rivers and constructed water-mills; they set up iron foundries and factories for making glass and other items; and, above all, they planted orchards and vineyards. St. Remi's will gives us some evidence for this: one of the properties he left to novices, priests and the serf who had cultivated it, was a "vineyard on the outskirts of Reims". One vineyard, founded at about that time at the Abbey of St. Thierry, near Reims, is still being cultivated by monks today, and vineyards were listed with details of acreage, production and numbers of workers in a late ninth century account book for the Abbey of St. Remi. Of those workers specifically named, the vintner came as high on the list as the fisherman and the cook – these three were clearly felt to be the most

important elements of the workforce.

There is plenty of contemporary evidence that underlines the involvement of religious houses in the cultivation of vines and the production of wine. One of St. Remi's successors as Bishop of Reims was Hincmar, in about 850AD. Hincmar wrote to his colleague, the Bishop of Laön, who had fallen ill, recommending "the mediocre wines of Epernay" as an aid to digestion, and to "drive out humours". Hincmar became very powerful as Archbishop of Reims, and had the support of the Pope in a row with Charles the Bald, the King of the West Franks and Holy Roman Emperor, over Charles' confiscation of church-owned monastic vineyards. In his complaint he listed hundreds of monastic vineyards. (In fact, half the vineyards in Champagne belonged to the monks in those days.)

Continuing instability

The productive life of the monks continued against a background of political unrest as Clovis's sons divided up his empire between them. Chaotic quarrels among the brothers ensued, but finally Clotaire II, a grandson, reunited the kingdom. From then on the story of the area was a complicated succession of political divisions and consolidations.

In 732AD Charles Martel, son of Pepin II, beat back an Arab invasion force that had reached Tours, thus "saving Christian civilization" (for more warring!), and became king in 741AD. His famous great-grandson, Charlemagne, built up enormous power, and combined all of France in his "Holy Roman Empire". Charlemagne governed by a system of "Counts" who ruled with princely splendour over various parts of his realm. He delegated local authority to them, as well as to bishops and abbots, who themselves built up fighting units to protect their holdings. Hugh Capet was one of these Counts, but not content with this, he was working with the Archbishop of Reims to get himself "elected" king. Capet claimed that a king should not inherit the crown, but obtain it through his own personal merit. His rival, Charles de Basse Lorraine, came to the Champagne capital to dispute Capet's rights. Hugh, an able, clever man and no stranger to questionable political tactics, persuaded the Bishop of Laön to arrest Charles while he

slept and then to turn him over to Capet.
Capet promptly imprisoned him at Orléans,
where he died. Capet was crowned in Reims
on the 3rd of July 937AD, a date that
marked the beginning of a new line of kings.
He died in battle in 1037.

Political power games
After Capet there was a series of wars of
succession between the Dukes of Anjou and
of Blois, the king and the Holy Roman
Emperor. Each kept in close touch with the
clergy, who were almost equally powerful,
and very much involved in political affairs.
Because of the nobility's rapacious greed,
the extraordinary marriages between
powerful feudal families (agreed on an
entirely "business" basis that could involve
whole regions), and the fact that there was
very little trust, even between members of a
family, Champagne, and indeed all France,
continued to endure political unrest.

**St. Bernard with his Cistercian monks at
the abbey of Clairvaux, which he
founded in 1115. St. Bernard was a
deeply religious mystic and reformer who
became embroiled in politics during the
Crusades.**

Politics became deeply complex with
sovereigns absent at the Crusades, sudden
deaths, intermarriages and treachery. While
the pride of Champagne's nobility went off
to fight in the Crusades they often left their
lands in much more intelligent, but often
more unscrupulous hands.

In the early 12th century, this situation
was still much the same, and the Church
wielded enormous power – largely because
of the general social unrest. Even the most
spiritual men became involved in temporal
affairs, the religious wars in the Holy Land
adding zest to their Christian fervour and

winning them popular support. The mystic and reformer, St. Bernard (1090–1153) was one of these men. He was simultaneously advisor to the Papacy and the founder of the Cistercian Order. He also founded an abbey, Clairvaux, in Champagne in 1115, near Bar-sur-Aube in one of the region's best vineyard areas.

St. Bernard, a deeply religious and remarkably persuasive man, was busily promoting his Second Crusade (1147–1149). One of the politicians he persuaded to go to battle the Saracen was Count Henri II of Champagne, who left for Palestine and Acre. Henry never came home because somehow he managed to fall out of a window in Acre and break his neck. His death, of course, changed the political picture in Champagne. It gave the Church a golden opportunity to become a temporal, as well as spiritual, counsellor to Henri's window. As a result, the Bishop of Reims became Champagne's true ruler, mingling with verve in the maze of temporal, religious and physical relationships – all in the pursuit of power – that made up political life at that time.

The domestic scene

During the Crusading period, noble ladies who had been abandoned by their husbands for the Holy Wars sometimes grew lonely and sought friends to keep them amused. One of the most famous of Champagne's lonely countesses was Marie de France, Countess of Champagne. She was the daughter of King Louis VII and Eleanor of Aquitaine, and was endowed with an intellectual and creative prowess that marked her out from contemporary women. Left behind by her Crusading husband, Count Henri II, she took to writing ballads for troubadors and encouraged other writers to support her ideas about what has become famous as the philosophy of "Courtly Love". So Champagne was the source of the "language of love", long before the romantic sparkling wine was tasted.

One of Marie's protegés was Chrétien de Troyes, who wrote the first Lancelot poem to her instructions in about 1120. Linked by later writers to the Celtic legends of King Arthur, the story was based on Marie's ideas that love was absolute, defined as a "certain inborn suffering", and, unfortunately for the moralists, impossible

The tale of the hopeless love of the monk, Pierre Abelard, for his pupil, Heloise Fulbert, has enchanted people throughout the centuries. Heloise became pregnant and her enraged father punished Abelard by castration. The unhappy man fled to Provins where Count Thibaud II of Champagne offered him protection and helped him to join a monastery, where he became abbot. Eventually he managed to bring his beloved Heloise to Champagne where he installed her as abbess in the nearby convent of Paraclet. It was only after Abelard's death in 1142, when Heloise brought his body to Paraclet, that the lovers were reunited. After the French Revolution, both their bodies were transferred to Paris's prestigious Pierre Lachaise cemetery.

between man and wife. Secrecy was an essential element of a love affair, as was a knight's slavish obedience to his lady's wishes. Venus, Cupid and Love were all sublimated for the glory of God through this "pure love". No external concerns, such as a dowry or a marriage, need interfere with its supposed purity of purpose. The radical philosophy of Marie de France established a wonderful romantic tradition throughout European literature.

Conflict and change

For almost 200 years between 1098 and 1270, Europe – not least the Champagne country – was bled dry by the eight Crusades that drained the population of some of its bravest and most noble citizens. The distant fighting in the Holy Land did mean that local warring simmered down, however, and Champagne gradually became far better off; indeed it was almost a wealthy country, lying, as it did, at the cross-roads of important trade routes between east and west, and north and south. Huge farming and industrial fairs were held at Troyes, Lagny, Provins and Bar-sur-Aube, which became rich on international trade and banking and remained so until the 13th century.

Once the Crusades were over, however, the old local friction returned with a vengeance. The wartime way of life had to change, and many people suffered as a result. Those who had been placed temporarily in important positions were often confronted by the threat of ruin when their predecessors returned from the Holy Land. Rival claimants for property, and the positions accompanying it, quarrelled fiercely. The proliferation of feudal, temporal and religious lords, both because of such duplication, and because those who had stayed at home had become wealthy enough to support their own armies, once more led to constant and vicious bickering.

Champagne was, of course, a cross-roads for invaders and warriors, as well as for commerce. The 100 Years War, from 1337 to 1453, particularly affected the region – whether it was the English against the French, or internecine civil war in France itself. The region was particularly badly hit by the War, since it became the battlefield for many confrontations between the English and French forces. Its commercial health suffered severely, but even during the fighting, wines from the Champagne region were still being floated down the Marne to Paris and transported by the wagon-load to Belgium. Two hundred years later, still Champagne wines, (both red and white), were considered good enough to compete with those of Burgundy for the French markets.

Wine by the barrel

They were powerful drinkers in those days. At the *sacre* of Philip VI of Valois in 1328, the guests downed 300 "pièces" of wine (containing 500 bottles each), of which part was from Beaune, part from Saint Pourcain and part from Champagne (the cheapest of the three). But the quality of Champagne's wines continued to improve. Later, at the *sacre* of Francis II, Champagne and Burgundy cost the same. Later still, at the crowning of Henry III, the cost of Reims wines surpassed even Burgundy's prices.

In 1518, the French Admiral de Bonnivet wrote to his friend Cardinal Wolsey in London that 20 barrels of Ay wine were en route to him as a gift. Another admirer of Champagne living in England was the French emigré Charles de Saint Evremond, who claimed that the Medici Pope, Léon X, King Charles V of France, and Henry VIII of England had all owned properties in or near Ay, so that they could count on their own supplies of the still white wines of Ay "not the least of their preoccupations", as he put it.

Nevertheless, except for the celebrated Ay, Champagne's wines were not that widely known at the end of the 16th century. During the 16th century, Champagne had to contend with the Religious Wars. Since Reims was mainly Catholic, it was at the centre of local disturbances, while Meaux, on Champagne's outer perimeter, was a Protestant enclave of Huguenots. The famous Roman quarries, the *crayères* used for storing today's Champagnes, were often put to service as hiding places by the Protestants of the Reims area.

In the 17th century however, the wines really began to come into their own, even though the countryside was a huge military encampment for most of the Thirty Years War between Spain, (fighting not only on the Mediterranean coast but also for its occupied possessions in the Low Countries bordering Champagne), and the Hapsburgs, against Louis XIII and Louis XIV of France. The Peace of Westphalia (1648) engineered by Cardinal Mazarin, finally left France and its Allies in control of Champagne. This uneasy peace brought some respite in the fighting and Louis XIV was crowned in Reims. Unfortunately, Louis had a naturally bellicose streak and he continued to fight the Dutch, the Germans and the Spanish until his death in 1715. Although he was successful, he exhausted France's economy.

There was little actual fighting in

Champagne during the 17th century, but the locals were pillaged and had their produce requisitioned by Louis XIII's troops stationed in the area. Then came 30 more years of riotings and confusion during the civil war of the "Fronde" between the king and Parliament, a foretaste of what was to happen in the French Revolution. Terrible damage was also done to Champagne when the Grand Condé stationed his undisciplined troops (foreign mercenaries from Sweden, Poland and Germany) in the towns and villages.

The mystery of Champagne unfolds

Against this background of political friction, the monks of Champagne were learning about the treatment of vines and wines. It was during this period that they and other *vignerons* discovered how to make white wine from red grapes. Champagne vineyards were producing only still wines, both red and white. The reds were not very red, more onion-skin, or partridge-eye coloured, a little darker than present day rosé, but not red. They were known as *clairet*, and were rarely good. In about 1700, the Champagne vintners began to realise that their white wines were better when made with as little contact with their lees (the deposit left in them by yeasts) as possible, and began to siphon wines from one barrel to another to avoid this. They also learned that high vines of up to 1.5m (5ft) produced quantity, while low vines, at about 1m (3ft) produced quality. They discovered that light pressing made for better wines, and that grapes should be picked in the cool of the day, not in the sun – in fact, preferably in fog or mist – and that mules used for ploughing did less damage to vines than donkeys or horses.

In the early years of the 18th century, the Wars of the Spanish Succession again affected the Low Countries and Alsace, Champagne's neighbours, threatening to disrupt the fabric of the Champenois' lives once more. But the monks were not to be deterred. Working in islands of peace during the mayhem they could, as they had for centuries, experiment on improving their wines. They considered this important because wine was an essential part of the sacrament and produced income for their abbeys; this is not to say that they did not keep a drop or two to enjoy for themselves!

As a result, they became the oenologists of their day, and knew more about making wine than most of their lay contemporaries. First of all they had the time; second, they were supported financially by their congregations and churches; and third, they gradually also became businessmen, and did a booming trade in their best vintages.

Hautvillers – the turning point

Among the most innovative of these "scientists" were two men of the same Abbey – Hautvillers – in Champagne, near Epernay. One was the celebrated Dom Pierre Pérignon, (1639–1715), the other his friend and contemporary, Dom Thierry Ruinart (1657–1709). Dom Pérignon is often described as the "inventor" of Champagne, but it seems more likely that

he was simply the first wine expert to apply contemporary knowledge in an effective way. There seems to be no written reference, either in his diary, in the records of Hautvillers, or even in its wine inventory, to the discovery of sparkling wine. A discovery as astounding as that would surely have excited some comment!

The abbey of Hautvillers (*below*) where the celebrated Dom Pérignon (*left*) was cellar master from 1668 to 1715. It was in the cellars of Hautvillers that the Dom discovered how to promote and control the effervescence in wine, and thereby launched the mass production of sparkling Champagne.

But the important thing to remember is that Champagne was never "invented" as such. Effervescence in wine is a *natural* phenomenon. Any wine-producing areas in which the sudden cold of the winter petrifies the activity of the yeasts in the grape juice, so that the complete conversion of the sugar into alcohol and carbon dioxide is delayed until the spring, will discover that their wines develop a sparkle.

In the early days of the wine industry, the fact that wine tended to fizz during

The Sun King, Louis XIV (1643-1715), was renowned for his love of Champagne wines, particularly those from Ay. It was only at the end of his life that his habits changed when he was advised by his physician that drinking only the wines of Burgundy would be better for his health.

fermentation was well established, but no-one fully understood the mechanics of this process. People enjoyed these sparkling wines, but the producers could not satisfy the demand because they were unable to guarantee the presence, or, more importantly, the duration, of bubbles in a wine. Another practical problem was that the sparkle in the wines was hard to control. Without understanding how the gas was produced by the wine, it was impossible to regulate its potency and often a too powerful fermentation would burst the impractically fragile glass of the bottles. The wine-makers were obsessed with the need to find a way to accommodate these two considerations.

Champagne has the perfect climate for creating effervescence in wine and Dom Pérignon had ample opportunity to study the process in detail. He did not "discover" the sparkle; he simply applied contemporary methods to control and contain it. Strangely enough, the credit for discovering the best way to control the fizziness of a wine must go to the English. François Bonal, in his definitive book "Champagne", describes how the English in 1662 added molasses and sugar to still wines to make them effervescent. English wine suppliers were also using bottles made of thicker glass to hold these sparkling wines, and had been using corks, (probably from Spain or Portugal), for many years to seal ordinary bottles. It would seem that Dom Pérignon heard about the efficiency of their methods and, realising how appropriate they were to the controlling of effervescent wines, he adopted the use of bottles made of *verre anglais* and Spanish corks in Champagne.

Rising popularity

There is a wonderful tale of how the delicious wine made its way to the table of Louis XIV at Versailles. Saint Simon tells an amusing, though perhaps apocryphal, story about the "Jolie Baronne", Jeanne de Thierzy, a young lady of Champagne who was married to a fanatical warrior, more often on the battlefield than at home and hearth. She did not hesitate to take advantage of his absences to satisfy her appetite for amorous adventure.

Every time she sinned, however, she would confess to the nearest priest, who happened to be Dom Pérignon. He, too, had his passion – wine. Finally he objected to his lovely parishioner, "You sin so frequently, and with so little remorse, that I find it impossible to go on forgiving you."

The Jolie Baronne cried so pitifully that the soft-hearted Dom relented and gave her absolution. Although she went straight back to her former peccadilloes, she did feel an obligation to Dom Pérignon for his understanding. She would show her gratitude by getting the king, Louis XIV to use the Dom's newly bubbling Champagne at Court.

Not long thereafter, the Maréchal François de Créqui, Duke of Lesdiguières, an officer serving with her husband, the Baron de Thierzy, in Holland, was sent through Epernay with dispatches for Versailles, and was charged by the rather naïve de Thierzy to say "hello" to his wife en route.

The Maréchal duly stopped by, and the Baronne found the visit just what she needed. She plied the willing soldier with several flagons of Dom Pérignon's best wine of Hautvillers. He not only appreciated the wine, but was much impressed with the beauty of his young hostess. He decided to tiptoe into her bedroom that night to see if he could improve on their relationship. The poor Maréchal was no Don Juan. He was fat, asthmatic, and had a red nose. But the Jolie Baronne, not a woman to be astonished at such behaviour, decided this was her opportunity. She pretended to be offended and shooed him out.

The next day, after bidding him goodbye, she climbed into his carriage. "I'm sorry I treated you so cavalierly last night," she said, "but I attributed your conduct to the wine you appeared to enjoy. Actually, it is one of my favourite wines. I think it should become better known at Versailles. If you can manage to get it used by the King, you *might* find it possible to obtain from me what you seemed so anxious to have".

At that moment, one of her servants thrust a case of Dom Pérignon's wine into the Maréchal's carriage, and off he trotted, delighted to have made such an impression on his charming hostess.

At Court, the Maréchal became the most persuasive of salesmen. Louis XIV was delighted with the wine, and ordered that the Abbey of Hautvillers should at once reserve a large part of its production for the Royal table.

The Maréchal could hardly wait to obtain permission to "return to his troops".

He galloped back to Epernay, where Jeanne kept her side of the bargain.

But when the Maréchal asked her for the secret of the wine's sparkle, she dropped her eyes and demurely protested, "Allow me to keep that secret, since I have revealed all my others." The Jolie Baronne felt she had found the ideal way to repay the good Dom for his absolution. "An eternity without pain", she thought, "is worth one night of love without pleasure".

The victim of war
Even during the French Revolution, the Champagne area was not allowed to rest from foreign war. In 1792, Austrian and Prussian armies advanced into France, determined to rescue Louis XVI and Marie-Antoinette, his Austrian queen, from the hands of the French revolutionaries. The Prussian king, Frederick William IV, was reluctant to join the venture, however, because he feared that Catherine the Great of Russia would seize the opportunity of expanding into Poland at Prussian expense.

As it turned out, Frederick William was right. The rescuing army advanced into France as far as Valmy, near the Argonne forest, whose heights gave it a fine view of the rolling Champagne countryside. There, a hastily-mustered French force forced their enemy to retreat, so saving Champagne from being overrun. Catherine took the opportunity of invading what remained of Poland, so Frederick William pulled out of his alliance with Austria to "concentrate on Polish affairs".

Though Valmy was little more than a skirmish – only about 500 men were killed or wounded on both sides – the battle was psychologically important to the French. It meant the survival of the Revolution. The First Republic was proclaimed two days later; a year later, both Louis XVI and his ill-fated queen were sent to the guillotine.

So the Champagne area was no stranger to military activity, as you can see. Napoleon himself spent some time there as

Champagne workers planting new vines in a traditionally haphazard pattern across the vineyard. Nowadays, vines are planted in regular rows for easy management. Note the depth of the exposed chalky subsoil of the mountain in the background.

a student at the royal military school, just north of the Var-sur-Aube vineyards from 1779 to 1784. Later, as he tried to defend his throne in 1814, he fought some memorable battles in the area, from which, as usual, the Champenois suffered. On his fall, the region was occupied by the victorious Austrian, Prussian and Russian "allies" for two years.

Champagne suffered again in 1870, when Napoleon III lost a new war against Prussia and her allies of the North German Confederation. In 1914, it was the scene of the famous "taxi" battle of the Marne, when General Gallieni, the Military Governor of Paris, rushed reinforcements to the front in taxis and trucks taken from the streets of the city to help halt the German drive on the nation's capital. The Germans were forced to retreat to the Aisne river, with their front lines finally being established just west of Reims and Epernay. There they remained for the rest of the war. It was in this region that General Nivelle launched the flower of France in a futile offensive against the German positions in 1917; such was its cost that the spirit of the French Army was nearly broken, many units mutinying and threatening to march on Paris to put a stop to the war.

The First World War was especially disastrous for Reims. The entire city centre was destroyed by protracted German long-range bombardment; by the time the war came to an end in November 1918, there were only 50 habitable houses left in the city.

The roof of Reims Cathedral caught fire in 1913 as a result of the German bombardment. It was constructed from huge oak beams and covered in lead. Once the fire caught hold, the devastation was uncontrolled.

Many of Reims' citizens spent most of the war years sheltering underground in the city's deep wine cellars. The front was only a few kilometres to the east, just beyond the Montagne de Reims. During that period, 15–16,000 shells fell on the city almost daily: Pommery's cellars actually ran under "no man's land". One of their corridors could hold over a thousand troops and had wells for water as well as tanks for drinking and washing water. It was said that 34 battalions – up to 60,000 men – could be accommodated if necessary in Champagne's cellars, which helped to discourage attacks!

In the Second World War, the Germans occupied both Reims and Epernay, and denuded their wine cellars. Whole trainloads of Champagne were sent off to the German troops. Strangely, the Wars' disruption did not seem to affect the wines. The 1914 vintage, for instance, was considered one of the best of the century. Vineyards kept on being tended carefully despite a hail of shells. Cellar owners, too, managed to preserve a good deal of their stock by hiding bottles behind false cellar walls. Not long ago, one firm discovered an antique Citroën car that had been walled-up and forgotten in a *cave*.

Not all the bombing in the region was entirely indiscriminate. Under the village of Rilly, on the Montagne de Reims, where some of Champagne's best vines grow, there is a tunnel of the commuter railway line between Epernay and Reims, about one-and-a-half miles long. "During World War II," a local informant told me, "the Germans blocked off both entrances to the tunnel, re-routed trains (if any) by a longer route, and stowed their V2 rockets there." The tunnel was, of course, almost ideal for hiding and protecting these long, highly conspicuous weapons. "The Resistance knew a little about what was going on," my friend said, "and tipped off the RAF. So Rilly got its share of heavy bombing even though no-one knew exactly what was going on there."

The new threat
It is not only man-made disasters that have struck Champagne and its wine-making industry. An even more lingering problem hit Champagne in the shape of a small bug, sometimes called a plant louse and sometimes less unattractively, an aphid. These insects, the phylloxera, which came close to destroying Europe's wine trade, did not exist in Europe until some time in the mid-19th century.

In the "good old days", before the insects arrived in Europe, they lived on American wild vine roots, safely on the other side of the Atlantic. Unnamed, experimental vintners, in about 1840, brought some American vines to Europe in innocence of the fact that they had also brought a plague with them. The fresh, luscious European vine roots had no resistance at all to the bugs that attacked their new, succulent food supply with delight. The results were disastrous. Once the phylloxera had begun to reproduce, it took them only about 20 years to almost completely annihilate the French vineyards and partially to wreck those of Spain, Italy and even Germany.

Eventually it was concluded that the only cure was to graft European wines on to immune American roots. At first, Champagne growers thought they would escape the blight. They violently resisted anti-phylloxera measures. "The aphids wouldn't dare attack such well-kept vineyards", the farmers claimed and they refused to inject their soil with insecticides.

The Champenois also adamantly refused to pull up their treasured vines and replant their vineyards with American roots, on which they would then have to graft their vines, on the grounds of expense.

Unfortunately the phylloxera were not listening. By 1898 the pest had reached the Champagne area. Only 13 years later, some 12–13,000 acres were affected – half the existing Champagne vineyards. Because of the way the Champagne business is organized, growers (commerçants) and distributors (négociants) were at odds as to the action they should take. The businessmen-distributors wanted to fight the bug by pulling up old plants. The growers thought these négociants were trying to get all the plantings into their own hands. Finally, the two parties, faced with a danger neither could avoid, reluctantly joined forces and began to replace the old vines with those that had been grafted on to resistant roots. By the start of the Second World War, about a third of the infected vines had been replaced.

A new tradition
The replanting brought about a revolution in the way grapes were grown. The old system of planting in Champagne had been chaotic. Plants were grown in a semi-natural state, like trees in a forest. To handle the new grafting it was easier to plant the vines in rows. This proved much simpler to manage, because horse-drawn weeding and spraying apparatus could be used between the lines. Better yet, the grapes got more sunshine, being farther apart, and they ripened better. But then, of course, the War came and working the vineyards became not only harder but actually dangerous.

This was the first great change in the way traditional Champagne had been handled in the vineyards. The second great change came later, after the Second World War, when the Champenois decided that too many sparkling wines outside the legally restricted Champagne region were taking this exclusive name in vain. The Champagne growers and distributors instituted legal proceedings to establish that there is no "Champagne" but Champagne, grown, picked, crushed, fermented, bottled and prepared for marketing in the officially "designated area" of Champagne, France.

Regulating the Industry

Champagne benefits from a unique structure as regards its production and its sales. For centuries it was made and sold, as were most French wines, by the same farmer-producer-proprietor. Land owners whose soil did not allow for top quality grape growing tended to plant vines that produced cheap, high yields, gaining in quantity what they could not give in quality. The wines produced in Champagne were prolific but of a standard that was not uniformly high. It was not until the major producers began to work with the small holders that Champagne's reputation as a quality wine could be established and maintained.

The neatly regimented rows of Chardonnay grapevines at Cramant, one of the famous *grand cru* villages of the Côte des Blancs, are filled with workers enjoying the sunshine at harvest time.

The early days

Before the French Revolution, the businessmen, (*les bourgeois*), the clergy and the nobility, were the only people who made and promoted Champagne wines. After the Revolution, the wine trade opened up and merchants began to develop markets, not merely in France, but abroad. They were not just salesmen – they bought still wines and turned them, or allowed them to turn, into sparkling ones because those sold at premium prices. Among the earliest well-known names of such merchant-producers, or *négociants*, were Ruinart and Moët in Epernay, and Clicquot and Heidsieck in Reims.

Merchants began to be more and more important in the 18th century, with such new names as Mumm, Mercier, Pommery, Pol Roger, Deutz, Ayala, Bollinger and Perrier emerging to join in the fun. Partly because they had built up enough wealth to be able to invest in the best equipment of the time, (not to mention the best vineyard locations), the merchant-producers were often far more successful than those who supplied them with the raw materials (grapes, or even wine) for blending Champagne *cuvées* – the farmer-producers, or *vignerons*.

These farmers could never be sure of what prices they would get for their hard work, especially since the merchants were inclined to import grapes from other areas even as far away as Algiers and make them into "Champagne", to the detriment of Champagne's own local vineyarders. The situation finally resulted in a revolt of the grape growers who demanded that the law restrict the name "Champagne" to wine made from grapes from "La Champagne", the region.

The basic problem of the *appellation* Champagne was solved in 1911 by a law decreeing that Champagne must be made with grapes from a legally fixed zone: the Montagne de Reims, Vallée de la Marne and Côte des Blancs areas. This did not put an end to the matter, however, because there were two areas of vineyards around Bar-sur-Aube and Bar-sur-Seine that had traditionally been suppliers of grapes to Champagne makers, but were not included in the newly delimited zone. Wine farmers there could see their livelihood disappearing at the stroke of a pen. More riots ensued,

A relic from the earliest days of the Champagne industry, this is the oldest bottle of Claude Moët's Champagne in existence. It dates from 1741, two years before the company was founded.

causing a new project for settlement to be proposed. Then the First World War intervened and the people had other things to worry about, but eventually agreements were signed allowing the southern vineyards to be considered as Champagne *appellation* after all.

Uniting the professions

The misunderstandings between producers and salesmen made it clear that Champagne depended on two different professions. The producers could not exist without the farmers, and the farmers could not sell their own product profitably without the sales organizations. Thus, realising they could not work efficiently without each other they finally agreed to agree, and in 1935, the first law defining Interprofessional Co-operation was promulgated.

Again War intervened. This time it was under supervision from the German occupation authorities that the two sides in the Champagne war got together during September 1941, in what was to become the *Comité Interprofessional du Vin de Champagne*, or CIVC. The infant organization included representatives from the *négociants* and from the *vignerons*, both reporting to a Vichy government minister, known as the "*Fuehrer du Champagne*". A semi-public body, the CIVC was set up to represent the common interests of the industry's two "professions" in co-operation with the government.

One of its founders was one of the most remarkable and imaginative men of the Champagne world – Robert-Jean de Vogüé. He represented the producers, while a co-founder, Maurice Doyard spoke for the vineyard owners. In its infancy, because Champagne was in German occupied territory, the Committee had to work with, and get around whenever possible, the restrictions imposed on the industry by the occupying power. It was the Comte de Vogüé's responsibility to liaise between the Germans and the resentful Champagne makers. He had to be a master of resistant diplomacy! The Champenois manufactured a variety of cunning ways to sabotage the German monopoly of their wines and the representatives of the CIVC tacitly encouraged them. Unfortunately, De Vogüé's luck ran out towards the end of 1942, when he was imprisoned in a concentration camp for the duration.

The CIVC today

The CIVC that has developed out of this wartime co-operation is an organization of professionals, as "democratic" as it is possible to make it, supple but authoritarian at the same time. It is composed of growers, both those who make their own wines and those who do not, and of merchants – again those who own vineyards as well as those who do not. Thus a member may, in some cases, belong to both "professions" if he chooses. The CIVC's personnel and expenses are paid out of fees received from the "professions", plus some government funds. The organization is therefore semi-official and semi-public.

CIVC's decisions are mandatory for all its members. They cover economic measures, production and marketing, raw material supplies in case of need, price structures, quality control and enforcement of its regulations. The Champagne producers recognize the value of its laws.

The cost of luxury

One of its trickiest jobs is to fix the prices of the grapes just after the harvest ends each year – the main source of friction between growers and producers in the past. The agreed figures are based not on the quality of the grapes themselves, but on what their juice turned into wine can be expected to fetch on the market. The growers' representatives, the producers and the CIVC officials base their pricing decisions on what a finished bottle of Champagne fetched in the preceding year. In this way they can determine minimum and maximum fixed prices for the grapes.

In conjunction with this procedure, the CIVC have classified all the Champagne vineyards according to the consistent quality of the grapes they produce. A maximum price is established for the best grapes, and the prices for the produce of all the other vineyards are calculated from this peak downwards. The grapes used for the most prized *crus*, for example, fetch 100 per cent of the agreed price for that category.

In this fashion the *vignerons* and the *négociants* are given a reference point from which to calculate the price for that year's crop. They can negotiate their own price between 10 per cent above or below the price officially fixed for their grapes. This allows for orderly buying and selling, whether a crop has been abundant *or* unusually small.

Vineyards that are growing "noble" grapes, like Chardonnay, Pinot Noir and Pinot Meunier, enjoy a slight premium on their offerings of those specific grapes. Although all of Champagne's vineyards have been classified according to the quality of their grapes on this 100 per cent scale, their grapes' quality must reach a minimum of 80 per cent, if the *cru* is to be considered worthy of becoming Champagne wine.

Seventeen *grand cru* areas have been given a price rating of 100 per cent. The villages that can ask 100 per cent of the fixed price are those of Ambonnay, Avize, Ay, Beaumont-sur-Vesle, Bouzy, Chouilly, Cramant, Louvois, Mailly-Champagne, le Mesnil-sur-Oger, Oiry, Puisieulx, Sillery, Tours-sur-Marne, Verzenay and Verzy. And there are 37 *premier cru* villages where the produce of the vineyards is rated at 90–99 per cent.

Under the present system of ratings, more than half the vines cultivated in the *grand cru* villages are Chardonnay. Most of the rest are growing Pinot Noir. The *cru* titles only apply to the noble grapes grown within village limits. The pricing structure is not applicable to any other types of grapes that the same villages may grow. In addition, both the *vignerons* and the *négociants* are required by contract to buy a certain quantity of grapes from their normal sources. In former days, a grower could refuse to sell his grapes for wine-making at all; or the merchant could – if his stocks were high – simply not buy.

Now, the quantity bought or sold is based on a percentage of the profit or loss made the year before, thus guaranteeing some continuity of purchases and sales. Contracts, of course, can be re-negotiated when they run out, but during their life they cannot be changed.

Naturally, there are agreements made in special circumstances when there is either a glut of grapes or a lack of them, but the system in general works to the satisfaction of both parties, and has certainly contributed to the stability of sales, profits and prices.

Technology for the future

The CIVC also provides viticultural services, including research laboratories and libraries, offering information about wine and the industry in general. It instigates quality checks and studies regarding disease and insect control. A great part of the Committee's resources are invested in technological research.

They have recently been investigating new methods of pressing grapes to improve the quality of the must. They have abandoned small presses, for example, in favour of bigger ones. A new "old-fashioned" wooden press that holds 4000kg (8800lb) of grapes at a time, is in the experimental stage and seems just right for Champagne grapes. The CIVC is also trying

to improve the vines themselves. Vines now being planted are chosen to be perfectly suited to the soil and micro-climates in which they are to be placed.

The Committee has its own experimental vineyards, a winery, and control laboratories that work hand in hand with the research and development staff of the co-operatives and of the bigger Champagne houses. A development that is causing a great deal of local interest regards the possible simplification of the traditional sediment-removing process.

Jointly undertaken by the Agronomical Institute of France, Moët et Chandon, and the CIVC, the procedure consists of encapsulating the yeast cells (that are a necessary part of the second fermentation process) in the bottle instead of letting them float free, as is done now. The yeast will be enclosed in a natural polymer bead, before being placed in the bottles. The spent yeast cells, once they have done their work of encouraging the second

fermentation, will be contained in the beads, which will subside in a solid lump, instead of as a free floating sediment, as is now the case.

Being denser than wine, the beads will collect easily and neatly onto the cork of an upended bottle, for removal in the usual way. The wine will not have to undergo expensive hand riddling, or the more efficient modern method of machine *remuage*, (*see Chapter V*).

Hopes for the method's efficiency are high, but proving that the method will not affect the wines as they age will require years of further testing. If the system works it will save a good deal of time and expense without in any way changing the quality or taste of the wines as they age.

Control throughout the industry

Of course, there are many other "professions" involved with the CIVC. The nurseries for the vines, the makers of presses and barrels, the manufacturers of modern machinery used in various processes, the bottle and cork makers, the cellarers, and the packaging and transport operators, all come under the CIVC's jurisdiction.

Champagne merchant-distributors realize that obtaining the very high standard of grape quality they need is an expensive proposition in terms of production. The growers, too, have discovered that they are not really able both to produce and sell their smaller private brands of Champagne efficiently, especially in export markets. So, they have joined forces to co-ordinate their respective activities, as efficiently and as economically as is possible in an industry that depends so much on climate. The CIVC supervises their activity in an advisory capacity. For example, with regard to the planting of vines, the CIVC insists that during planting, a balance is maintained between the varieties of grape that are used, in order to maintain traditional flavour and quality. They also

The vast circular wooden presses at Moët & Chandon's winery in Epernay. The traditional Champenois method of pressing grapes with such delicacy that their skins do not taint the colour of the must, is still employed.

supervise a sequential replanting of the old or weather-damaged vines over a period of 10 years.

When the plantings do reach the maximum area, (at least under the regulations now in force), average sales worldwide are expected to be kept at around the 250 million bottle level. To maintain such a figure will require a certain amount of "rationing" of supplies to the industry's world markets. The lucky recipients will have to be selected so that Champagne's exclusivity as a luxury wine is not undermined. But those who are excluded will undoubtedly be very unhappy. What will happen if demand continues to increase, (as it has over the past few years), is a question that the CIVC is pondering very seriously.

An ever-expanding market
The market for Champagne has shown a continuing rise, with occasional lapses during wartime, or during disputes between growers and shippers. But the graph of sales has shown a generally upward trend since the beginning of the industry in the early 19th century. For many years, the French home market has traditionally been Champagne's best; with Britain, the USA and Germany coming next in line. The first government figures solely for Champagne sales were compiled in about 1844. The total sales figure for sparkling Champagne in 1844–45 came to 6,706,799 bottles. Previously Champagne had been better known for its still red and white wines.

Figures for all the Champagne wines, regardless of the percentage of effervescent wines, show a total sale of only 36,820 bottles average per year during the years 1720–25. In 1788 these figures had only reached 288,400. It is obvious that adding the sparkle produced a sensational effect on wine sales over the next 50 years! By the turn of the 19th century, sparkling Champagne was selling at the rate of 28,454,436 bottles a year, of which nearly 22 million were exported. Some of this wine was made with grapes from vineyards other than those of the Champagne country. Just before the First World War, in 1912, however, delimited, official Champagne sales, had hit a total of 29,373,899 bottles. The war caused this figure to drop, but only to 26,544,632 bottles as recorded in 1914.

The quality of the wine remained high. The 1914 vintage was among the best of the century, and those of 1915 and 1917 were also excellent. While Reims was being attacked in 1918, the citizens promised the soldiers of a colonial division, who were defending them, two bottles of Champagne each every day as long as they kept the enemy out of the city. Happily the soldiers succeeded and managed to collect their delicious prize!

Shipments, however, dropped to a little over 10 million bottles in 1915. When peace was declared they rose again, in 1918, to over 17 million. America's declaration of Prohibition in 1922 caused a drop of some 9 million bottles. Just before the beginning of the Second World War, total sales hovered up and down between 18 million and 40 million bottles, not reaching the 40 million mark again until 1956.

From that date on, sales have been rising, with very few backslidings. The most recent figures available, those of 1986, show that over 200 million bottles were shipped. That was the best year since the overall record was set in 1983 to the tune of 159,500,000 bottles.

The 1986 figures prove that the French have patriotically supported their home industry by ordering 129 million of the total 204,920,108 bottles. The Anglo-Saxon communities (Britain, the USA, Canada and Australia) have valiantly tried to do their part by purchasing between them nearly 40 million bottles.

A group of four of Europe's smallest nations: Switzerland, Belgium, the Netherlands and Denmark, in that order, bought more than 13.5 million; and two of its largest, (apart from France, of course), Germany and Italy, together accounted for 15.6 million.

Success in spite of competition
What is even more surprising, when you think of the quantities involved, is that sparkling wines of all sorts have been jumping into the market in fierce competition with Champagne. In France alone, there are many excellent competitors. Possibly the first of these is the sparkling wine of Saumur, which is made from grapes grown south of the Loire river, in soil quite similar to that of Champagne, but from different grapes, usually Chenin

Before the laws were passed defining the factors which guarantee a true Champagne, there were many producers who used the famous name to promote their sparkling wines, to the irritation of the Champenois.

Blanc and Cabernet. In the South of France, Blanquette de Limoux, made near Carcassonne, claims to be an even more ancient "sparkler" than Champagne, while a comparative newcomer to the sparkling firmament, Alsace, now sells "Crémant d'Alsace" to the modest tune of four and a half million bottles yearly.

The Germans produce a sparkling "Sekt" in huge quantities, and American vineyards make sparkling *méthode champenoise* wines that compete locally. Perhaps the most successful of the competitors in terms of quantity were the Spanish who called their sparkling wines "Champana", until they were stopped by an historic lawsuit in 1960, brought by the CIVC and a group of the British importers of Champagne's 12 *Grandes Marques*. In 1973, France and Spain signed an agreement stating that

neither "Champagne" nor "Champana" could be used to name Spanish sparkling wines. They are now called "Cava".

According to new EEC regulations, even the term *méthode champenoise* will be illegal in a few years, for wines from other than the Champagne region. Some people think this is a mistake because the use of the words provides widespread publicity for the real thing, and immediately alerts the customers to the fact that the contents of the *méthode* labelled bottle is not *real* Champagne.

In the USA, laws about wine labelling are of course very very different. Any resemblance between a generically labelled US wine and its European namesake is rare. This is particularly true of Champagne. Thus, any sparkling wine in America can call itself "Champagne" although it may not be made with the same grapes, nor by the *méthode champenoise*, to say nothing of not being grown in the specific area of Champagne. The French, however, are investing in American vineyards quite heavily and they have to be particularly careful about the labelling of their wines. Some of the *Grande Marques* Houses are making good quality sparkling wines in California, but scrupulously avoid calling them Champagne.

A perennial favourite

It is obvious from these facts that the world consumer-public's taste for Champagne wine, or wines similarly sparkling, is continuing to expand. The reason why Champagne itself can keep up with this almost insatiable world thirst for "bubbly" is partly owing to its past problems with phylloxera and the disruption of war. For years a great many acres of authorized wine-growing land lay fallow because of anti-phylloxera measures. Out of the total area of some 35,000ha (86,485 acres) that is permitted to be used for Champagne grapes, around 10,000ha (24,710 acres) are still either under forest or uncultivated. At the end of the Second World War there were only 11,000ha (27,100 acres) under vine. Now there are some 27,000ha (66,720 acres) planted with vineyards. It is possible that, if demand continues to increase, about half of the present unplanted areas will be converted to vine growing by the year 2000.

From vineyard to market

Of the vineyards now planted, nearly three-quarters grow Pinot Noir and Pinot Meunier. A little more than a quarter of the total is planted with Chardonnay. This accords roughly with the traditional balance of grapes used in a Champagne cuvée. The vineyards are owned both by growers, of whom there are some 15,000, and by producers. Most of the growers own rather small plots of 1–5ha (2½–12 acres). Amazingly enough, only about 5 per cent of all the growers cultivate vineyards covering more than 4ha (10 acres) of land. The Champagne négociants usually buy their grapes from the vignerons. They shop around for the best quality and the best prices, unless they have a contract with a grower or growers for the purchase of a fixed quantity of their harvest each year. They tend to stick to the vignerons they have known and dealt with for years. Some of the smaller producers, however, often own relatively small vineyards and "declare a harvest" themselves. This means that they use the produce of their own vineyards to supplement the grapes they buy from the other growers. They use their grapes to

blend their own particular cuvée.

There are other vineyard owners who can almost be classified as gardeners. These récoltant-manipulants own small, but adequate vineyards where they produce their own wines, which they sell under their own label either at roadside stalls or by mail order. They frequently belong to co-opérative pressing and storage groups who handle these aspects of the wine-making process. Their output is inevitably variable, since it depends on the local mini-climate, but the small holders account for an astonishing 30 per cent of total Champagne sales – mainly within France. Driving through the Champagne countryside you often see signs urging you to stop, taste and buy these "private brands", sometimes at very reasonable prices. Many people discover a really excellent wine, but satisfaction is usually a matter of luck!

The major négociants account for 70 per cent of total sales of Champagne. Of the 110 Champagne Houses, the 10 biggest companies each sell over four million bottles of Champagne yearly – 62 per cent of all "Merchant House" sales.

The next 14 of the larger Houses each sell one million bottles or more (up to four million). Nine smaller Houses sell between half a million and a million; 17 sell from 200 thousand to half a million; and the rest between 10 and 200 thousand bottles.

The bigger Houses have their own trade association, called the "Syndicat de Grandes Marques de la Champagne", the smaller ones another association, the "Syndicat du Commerce des Vins de Champagne". Their joint meetings go under the name, "Union des Syndicats du Commerce des Vins de Champagne." The associations' task is to maintain quality control and adherence to the CIVC's regulations.

France is still by far the biggest customer for Champagne's produce. About two-thirds of the total is sold within the country, even though Champagne earns more foreign currency than any other great wine of France. Recently the USA has slightly caught up with Great Britain as Champagne's number one customer abroad.

The happiness and enjoyment promoted by indulging in the luxury of Champagne is depicted in this 1904 cartoon.

In the Vineyard

There is a good deal of conflicting information about how the grapevine found its way into the Champagne country. In the 19th century, many writers were claiming – often simply copying each other's ideas – that Julius Caesar and his armies were responsible for bringing the vine into northern Gaul. However, more serious scholarship doubts that the vine reached such chilly northern climes until considerably later.

Fossil vine leaves have been found near Sézanne, it is true. But these are something like the wild vines of North America – not suitable for making wine that pleases the palate. Various Roman laws, in the time of the emperors Domitian and Probus, proposed either destroying the vines of the "Provinces", or forbidding their being grown because they were over-productive and competed unfavourably with the home-grown products of Italy. These laws, as far as France was concerned, apparently referred only to southern Gaul – the vineyards located between Marseilles and the Pyrenees. These same vineyards are today once more producing so copiously that the area is blamed for being responsible for creating a "wine lake" of enormous size, in which some producers are likely to drown in the future.

Vines along the Mediterranean coast were planted first by Greek, and then by Roman colonists. They were gradually developed northwards to keep up with the expanding Roman power machine. From Provence the vines reached what is now the Burgundy region, and the Moselle, during the third century AD. Most authorities, including the official French governing body for the Champagne industry, the CIVC, seem to believe that the first wine-producing vineyards in Champagne only appeared between the third and fifth centuries AD.

Christianity – the catalyst

It was really the widespread establishment of Christianity that instigated the cultivation of vines in Champagne on a grand scale. The men of the religious houses were dedicated to the production of wine from their own grape harvests, to serve at Mass as well as at their own tables. Wherever there was an abbey, there would invariably be a lovingly-tended vineyard. Abbeys were springing up like mushrooms in the southern part of Champagne. The 12th century saw at least 14 Cistercian monasteries established in the Marne region alone, the Order being urged on to ever greater effort by the hypnotic enthusiasm of St. Bernard's preaching.

Eventually these, and other monasteries, became very well to do from the sales of their wines. The monks had plenty of time in which to experiment with and improve their methods of producing wine. The majority of vineyards of any size, and especially those making the best quality wines, were owned by either the monasteries or by the families of the nobility. For the bishops and the nobles, wine was a matter of prestige. There was constant social visiting between members of these noble families and the inmates of the abbeys. Hospitality was evaluated in terms of the "distinction" of the wines served. The Bishop of Reims owned prestige vineyards in both Reims and Epernay and was able to delight his guests with the high quality of his wines.

It was undoubtedly the monks of Champagne, like Dom Pérignon (*right*) and his Benedictine brothers, who were principally responsible for the development of the region's celebrated expertise in methods of wine production.

Survival against the odds

The various wars that broke out in France between the 14th and the 17th centuries brought Champagne nothing but trouble. During the Fronde, the main cause for grievance was the presence of foreign mercenaries in the region, stationed there by Louis XIII and later by Louis XV. These unruly soldiers marauded around the countryside wreaking havoc. The vineyards were neglected by the terror-stricken Champenois, and many were maliciously destroyed. These factors, combined with a long period of appalling cold, wet weather, threatened to cripple the wine industry.

Nevertheless, the middle of the 17th century saw some order restored and Champagne began to make fairly good red wines and some not so good white ones. There were a few excellent whites, however, which were able to rival even those of Burgundy. Champagne vintners began to be noted for taking unusual care of their vines and in the making of their increasingly popular wines.

Innovations in Champagne

Competition with Burgundy forced the Champenois to find means of making better and better white wines, since their vineyards were too far north for them to be

Working in the Champagne vineyards has been a tradition for the locals since the earliest days of the industry. The rhythm of their lives was governed completely by the seasonal changes in the vine.

able to make red in any quantity. They perfected a way to produce white wine from black grapes, a process till then little known. Patrick Forbes, in his comprehensive book "Champagne", suggests that Dom Pierre Pérignon was responsible for discovering how to press black grapes so delicately that they would produce still white wine. This white from black was of a far better quality than Champagne's white from white. In their earlier experiments, the Champenois had produced only a slightly off-white wine that was called *vin gris*, or depending on the depth of colour, such names as *oeil de perdrix* (partridge's eye), or *pélure d'oignon* (onion skin). The new "white from black" became very popular, and vineyards in the easier-to-work, flatter lands of Vertus, Sézanne, Châlons and St. Menehould, which had been producing "worthy" still, white and red wines, could not keep up with demand.

Until the beginning of the 17th century, Champagne was happy with the success of its still wines – red, white and *rosé*. But as the 18th century dawned, various knowledgeable wine experts were experimenting with sparkling wines, a phenomenon that was known, but uncontrolled. Sparkling wines were rare at this time, but greatly appreciated by the people who drank them. Louis XIV, of course, was known to drink only Champagne all his life, until his doctor told him that Burgundy was better for his health, a recommendation that did no harm at all to the fortunes of the Burgundians!

That irresistible sparkle

As I described in Chapter II, it was most probably the work of Dom Pérignon that established a profitable market in sparkling Champagne wines. He was also almost certainly responsible for introducing the pressing and blending methods, still employed in Champagne today, which guarantee a clear, pale golden white wine of a consistently high quality. With foresight and intelligence he combined his viticultural knowledge with contemporary discoveries to make sparkling white wine into a "practical" product, (*see pp.81–83*). His conviction of the potential of sparkling Champagne, was not misplaced – as subsequent events reveal.

The Champagne boom

The popular new sparkling wine was not without its detractors. In a document called the *"Journal des Etats tenus a Vitry-le-François en 1744"*, a certain Bertain de Rocheret writes: "Avize is a fairly big town that has grown tremendously in the past 12 to 15 years because of the frenetic invention of sparkling wine. Avize made a poor wine in 1719, their vines only producing a small, sour grape, with a flavour that gave it one of the tiniest reputations in the country. It sold for only 25 to 30 *livres* [pounds] per barrel. But since this mania for cork-popping, that abominable drink sells for 300 *livres* a barrel and an acre of vines that you couldn't sell for 250 *livres* now costs up to 2000." The escalating sales of Champagne proved the inaccuracy of M. de Rocheret's gloomy disapprobation! They also meant that new vineyards were hacked out of the forests that covered the slopes of the Montagne de Reims, especially between Reims and Epernay. Prices for these new lands rose by nearly 100 per cent between 1719 and 1744, yet people still rushed to cash in on the boom.

The clergy and the nobility, who controlled most of the more productive vineyards, were delighted with the popularity of the new wine. They became even more prosperous and extended their lands wherever they could, often at the cost of their tenants or employees. Even the independent farmers suffered from this monopoly. They were forbidden to own their own presses and had to take their grapes to those belonging to the local *seigneurs*, at great cost. Labourers eventually had little choice but to work for these landowners and they were exploited appallingly. The clergy were the principal employers just before the Revolution and they were notorious for their harsh treatment of those working on their lands. Not only were the workers ill-treated; they were also underpaid. Needless to say, this situation altered radically when the tide of Revolution broke.

The division of the spoils

The nobles and clergy lost all their possessions with the Revolution. In the Champagne country the losses were accompanied by far less violence than in some other parts of France. Nevertheless, one House that suffered was that of Madame la Maréchale d'Estrees, a very successful Champagne producer, who was hated by the peasants she employed.

Enormously wealthy, though apparently far from generous towards her employees, she bequeathed a huge quantity of wine to her heir, Charles Alexis Brulart, Comte de Genlis. He was caught during the Revolution, and his peasants took their revenge on the old Maréchale by ransacking the house and property. There is no account of what they did with her 71,650 bottle stock of Champagne, nor of her 500 *pièces* (barrels, each holding the equivalent of 288 bottles of wine). But it takes only a little imagination to guess that there was many a headache among members of her ex-staff, before the new government stepped in to requisition the vineyards, guillotine the Comte, and declare the estate national property.

The titles to feudal property holdings were revoked by the new popular government. The land was sold so that some *vignerons* could become owners. Many bought the vines that had belonged to the monasteries, or to members of the nobility who had fled abroad – the *emigrés*. Prices for land fell but most of the properties had been so extensively split up that each plot was really too small to be run profitably. Vestiges of those small holdings remain along the Marne and the Vesle rivers today.

This is the best vineyard growing area; houses are sprinkled amongst the tightly packed vineyards, like little islands surrounded by seas of vines. Sometimes the houses are grouped together amongst the vines, forming small but prestigious villages; there are some 250 of these communities. Separated from the conglomerations, the occasional "great house", or famous *château*, lies in its own park – monuments to some of the best known names in the world of Champagne.

Adapting over the years

The sprinkling of small plots of vines across the authorized area of Champagne has turned out to be an advantage in one sense. The dispersion allows different *vignerons* to compensate for their losses in one plot (because of micro-climatic differences) through the sales of their grapes from another. One section might be hit by frost or a hailstorm and destroyed: another could not only have escaped damage, but might even have enjoyed warm sunshine. Because Champagne is a blended wine, owning different plots also turns to advantage when harvests are poor. Wines made in previous years, possibly from better plots,can be mixed with those of off-years to produce very drinkable *cuvées*.

The perfect environment

Good wine depends on a good soil and, of course, on good grapes. The entire geographical territory included in Champagne is huge – stretching from near

Avize in the Côte des Blancs, seen here from Cramant, boasts Chardonnay vines that are rated at 100 per cent. It qualifies as one of the 17 prestigious *grand cru* villages.

Paris to the Meuse river that flows north into Belgium, and reaching from near Soissons down as far south as Bar-sur-Seine (*see p.13*). But of this comparatively vast area, only a tiny part (about a sixtieth) is actually planted with Champagne grapevines.

The majority of the best vineyards in this area are grouped around or near the Montagne de Reims – no Himalayas, or even Alps, the Montagne is really part of a plateau. The highest point of the whole region is only 378m (1200ft) above sea level. Champagne vines, which live for about half as long as humans, grow mainly in a narrow undulating strip of lovely farming country, winding along the banks of the various rivers, for some 215km (130mi). The vines spread out below the wooded hilltops mostly facing southeast or east. Some of the best, however, face north. The vineyards of Verzenay and Mailly, on the northern slopes of the Montagne de Reims, look towards the city, in little mini-climatic pockets, protected by the hills from the prevailing wind.

Champagne is just close enough to the Channel and to the Atlantic to benefit from some of their warming influences. The temperature can rise as high as 30°C (86°F) on a glorious summer day. The average summer temperature, however, is a mild 18.2°C (65°F), while winter temperatures average 3–4°C (37–40°F). This partly accounts for the surprising fact that, despite its northerly position, the vines of Champagne produce quality grapes, and with favourable weather conditions, they can produce more juice than the same quantity of grapes from some of the Mediterranean vineyards. Champagne is also blessed with a relatively dry climate. This does not mean that it escapes the occasional deluge. The rainiest month of the year is June and the Champenois can face enormous problems when the weather lives up to its reputation with unusual gusto. In June 1722, for example, a hailstorm raged so violently that it stripped all the grapes and the leaves from the vines over a substantial area of the countryside, and a similar June storm did equal damage in the Marne in 1971.

Some water is, of course, essential to growing vines, and the area has a plentiful supply. This was not always the case,

The distinctive church tower of Villedommange emerges from the sea of surrounding Chardonnay, Pinot Noir and Pinot Meunier grapevines, a proud landmark visible from many miles away.

In some areas of Champagne, the depth of the chalk subsoil is exposed. Both the insulating effect of this layer and its ability to retain moisture are essential to the survival of the vines.

however. In the 7th century Sainte Berthe founded a convent at Avenay without paying attention to the fact that it had a poor water supply. At the nearby, older abbey of Verzy, the monks had plenty of fresh water and Sainte Berthe persuaded them to agree to rent her the use of their spring for one *livre*. The problem which then arose was how to get the water from the spring two miles away at Vertuelle, to Avenay. Sainte Berthe solved this easily by inviting the spring to follow her to her convent. Legend has it that she walked away from the spring, trailing her distaff behind her, thereby automatically cutting a stream bed from Vertuelle to Avenay. The nuns have drunk pure spring water ever since; the little stream was christened *"La Livre"* ("The Pound") in honour of the rent paid by Sainte Berthe.

The topsoil in Champagne is fairly thin, varying from about 0.3m (1ft) to some 3m (10ft) in depth. The topsoil along the river valleys can reach as much as 30.5m (100ft) in depth due to the erosion from the hills. This thick layer is also the result of generations of vineyard enrichment from all the fertilizers and the mulch that has accumulated over the several hundred years of viticulture in the area.

Under the topsoil lies the famous bed of porous chalk which provides a constant supply of water for the vines. This 100 million-year-old base is made up of the bones and shells of ancient sea beasts, and also acts as a sort of under-floor warming system, retaining warmth and resisting cold for longer than ordinary soil. The result is an evenness of temperature favourable to vine growth.

It is this special quality of soil that makes Champagne's vines so unique – as the French say "There is no Champagne but from Champagne".

The laws of the vineyard

The grapes approved by the CIVC for use in making Champagne are limited to three main types: Chardonnay, Pinot Noir and Pinot Meunier. In fact every step of the wine-making process from the propagation of the vine through to the final *mise en bouteille* comes under the strict legislation passed on July 22, 1927. These original laws have been amended slightly over the years, but in essence they remain the same.

Only a strictly defined area of 35,000ha (86,487 acres) of the unique chalky soil of Champagne can be used for growing Champagne grapes. Of this area, some 27,000ha (66,718 acres) are actually under vine. No-one may plant new vines without authorization from the French Ministry of Agriculture. Even replanting can be done only if the vineyard owner is able to uproot the equivalent area of old vines within his own property; no re-planting is allowed outside specified parcels of land within each community or township.

Of the three approved grape varieties, Chardonnay grapes are slightly longer and thinner than Pinot Noir grapes, with rather small berries that become golden yellow or amber coloured when ripe. They tend to bud earlier than the two Pinots, which makes them vulnerable to frost in the spring. They grow best in the chalk soil of the Côte des Blancs and, with a warm growing period, become quite sweet, and can give freshness, elegance and delicacy to wines made from them.

The Pinot Noir grape is rather susceptible to cold weather. Its fruit is small, round, tightly packed and dark purple in colour, and it flourishes in a chalky soil. The grapes are tough and strong and produce what the French call a "fine bouquet".

The third grape, Pinot Meunier, is similar to Pinot Noir in shape, but its young leaves have a pinkish-white powdery look that gave it its name – supposedly being reminiscent of the colour of milled flour. It is better able to withstand bad weather than the Pinot Noir, and less delicate in taste. It gives a good quality, if less aristocratic, wine and ages faster than its hardy cousin.

All three types must be planted in rows that are not more than 1.5m (59in) apart, and there must be between 90–150cm (35½–59in) between vinestocks in the same row. The idea of spacing the vines is to allow each vine the optimum growth opportunity. If they were planted any closer together they would suffocate each other.

Guaranteeing success

Like farmers all over the world, the *vignerons* have their traditional prophetic sayings: "If November is thunderful, the year will be wonderful" or "March dry and hot, more wine in the pot"; or "June makes quantity, September makes quality"; and "August thunder brings fat grapes and good must in October". Hard-headed governments, however, cannot afford to put their faith in mere sayings when it

The noble Pinot Noir (*left*) and Chardonnay (*above*) are two of the grape varieties that are permitted for use in Champagne. The Pinot Meunier variety is less distinguished than its cousin, but also produces a fine wine. The production of three other noble grape varieties (Petit Meslier, Arbanne and Pinot Blanc Vrai) is on the decline.

comes to regulating the quality of the grapes. They prefer to impose limits on the pruning and the grafting of the vines. Grafting is undertaken to prevent the spread of phylloxera. The vines are grafted on to *porte-greffes* (rootstocks) of American origin, which are now grown in French nurseries. The rootstock keeps the vine free of phylloxera, (*see p.37*), because the aphid lives on but does not damage the American variety's roots. The graft supplies the nourishment for the healthy European branches, leaves and grapes without in any way introducing an "American" strain into the vinestock.

Grafting

Grafting in Champagne usually takes place in the laboratory because the climate of the region is too rigorous for regular grafting in the vineyards. It is largely undertaken by machine nowadays at the tremendous rate of 3000–4000 grafts a day. The prepared "clean" rootstocks are stored in the famous *crayères* until they are needed for grafting in the early spring. They are covered with fine sand to preserve their moisture content. In February, the cuttings which will be grafted on to these rootstocks are taken from the very best vines in the vineyard. Great care is taken to ensure that the cuttings and the rootstocks are compatible and that they are kept warm in the early stages, so that the graft "takes". Any that fail to do so are carefully eliminated.

During the cold spring freezes when the vines are particularly susceptible to frost, many producers spray the growing buds with water, ensuring their survival by sealing them within a case of ice.

The healthy grafted vines are kept in nurseries until the following November, when selected plants are put into bio-degradable pots, ready to be taken out into the cold, cruel world to begin their 30-year-long careers producing the essential ingredient of wine making, the grapes.

Nurturing the young vines

Once planted, the vine needs care – especially protection in winter against frost. One method is to keep spraying the buds during spring freezes with water, thereby coating them with a thin layer of ice. Within this little ice pocket the bud keeps warm enough to prevent it freezing and dying. The traditional, less effective way was to cover the vines with clouds of smoke, or to place braziers at strategic

points in the vineyard – a system that was found to be highly costly. Blowing hot air on to the vines is a third method that is often used.

Pruning

When the plants begin to grow branches and leaves, pruning becomes necessary if the plant is to produce the optimum quantity of grapes. It also allows the young grapes to receive both the maximum of sap from the main vinestock, and the greatest exposure to the sunshine. St. Vincent, the protector of wines and vines, is supposed to have got the idea for pruning from his donkey. According to local legend, the hungry animal strayed into the Saint's vineyards and set to work satisfying his hunger on the vines. He spurned the sour,

Training the vines on carefully placed wires was and still is an important part of work in the vineyards. If they are not trained, the profusion of shoots inhibits work between the rows.

undeveloped grapes to feed on the vine leaves. St. Vincent noticed later that the "damaged" vines produced a better crop than those that were left untouched, so he experimented with the judicious elimination of the apparently unnecessary sunshades.

Pruning takes place sometimes as early as January, although most Champagne growers will wait until the weather improves in March, and can even delay until April. Modern methods are being employed in this activity, with motor-driven cutting machines carried like a rucksack, instead of using secateurs as they did in the old, back-breaking, exhausting days of hand-pruning. Imagine each wine-grower having to clip two to five hundred thousand shoots by hand within about three months! It used to be thought necessary to remove the cut shoots, but today they are often left on the ground to provide enrichment for the soil.

Training the vines as close as possible to the wires on which they grow is also very important, to make weeding easier and allow soil-aerating tractors, and, of course, human grape pickers, to pass between the lines of grapes without damaging them. An untrained vine will grow shoots out in all directions and make the grapes very inaccessible.

Four traditional training methods are permitted: Chablis, Cordon, Guyot and Vallée de la Marne. Chardonnay and Pinot Noir vines should be pruned according to the Chablis method. This involves leaving the first branches only 60cm (24in) above the ground. Pinot Meunier vines are pruned to the Vallée de la Marne method, in which the first branch must not be more than 50cm (20in) from the ground. The vines are pruned this close to the ground so that they can benefit from the earth's retention of the sun's heat in these chilly northern Champagne latitudes.

In the spring, bulges begin to appear, at intervals, along the length of the vines' branches. Each bulge will always contain two leaf buds and one grape bud. Mother Nature arranges the buds so that of the two leaf buds, one immediately becomes a leaf, while its twin remains dormant for a whole year to produce the next new shoot. The twin leaf and the single grape bud are naturally arranged to be alternately facing the sky and the ground, so that the grape bud is never paired with a leaf that steals its sap or its sun. Nature's habits are, as always, extremely regular. But she still needs a vineyard owner to help her to produce her very best.

The hardworking *vigneron* has to reduce the number of branches ("the wood") so that the grapes on those that are left can get as much sap as they need. Generally, the more severe the pruning the better. The sugar content of the grapes increases, as does their capacity to produce the essential and highly desirable alcohol.

Until grafting was introduced in Champagne to prevent the spread of phylloxera, vines were propagated by layering — applying rooting hormones to the exposed vinestock bark to stimulate the growth of new roots.

Maintaining the soil

During the winter the topsoil between rows of vines is kept free of weeds, often using chemicals. The dirt is ploughed up into little ridges against the vinestocks. These ridges must be "unploughed" again in the spring. Both operations help to replace oxygen in the soil. This work is done by vine-straddling tractors, or, if the hillside is too steep for tractors, by a system of pulley-controlled ploughs.

I saw an interesting experimental treatment of soil at one of Champagne's most redoubtable vineyard *grand cru* terrains – Cramant, a pretty village on the Côtes des Blancs. To my utter amazement, the ground under the vines was littered with what looked like garbage – paper, china, corks, bottle tops, broken glass. And it was ploughed into the earth, not just scattered. It turned out that it *was* rubbish – from Paris. "Only from the best *arrondisements*, of course", said my guide with a twinkle. The rubbish is another inexpensive, if unattractive, means of helping to aerate the soil. Any broken glass

reflects the sun's heat, and the other bits and pieces bring in much needed oxygen by breaking up the solidity of Cramant's thick, sticky, clay topsoil.

The enemies of the vine

Besides being vulnerable to frost, hail and other inclement weather conditions, vines are liable to suffer from several kinds of fungal disease – the worst being mildew and oidium. These are prevented by spraying the vines with sulphates. Several other bacterial diseases can attack the vines, as well as enemies such as insects and birds. Migratory starlings, that sometimes arrive in huge clouds of a million birds or more, just as the grapes are ripe and ready for the harvest are particularly destructive. According to François Bonal, a million starlings can eat 31t (29 tons) of grapes a day! Using the birds' own danger-warning calls to scare them off is partially successful, but often they simply fly on to a neighbouring and less threatening vineyard to finish their meal.

Coming to fruition

Vines begin to come to life in the spring, just like any other plant. If the bulges on the branches are plump the *vignerons* say that "there must be plenty of grapes in them". When they open out, they put out shoots at the rate of about 5cm (2in) a day in good, warm, humid weather. Little tendrils reach out to catch on to the supports thoughtfully placed for them by the vignerons, and grow obediently on the training wires.

Vines can suffer from a variety of fungal diseases. The *vignerons* spray their crop with sulphates, to combat this problem. Modern farm machinery allows for speedy and extensive spraying.

Towards the middle of June, the vines flower and are fertilized mainly by bees or the breeze. Each flower is hermaphrodite and can both produce pollen and receive it. Pollen needs sunshine to dry it out so that it can be scattered by the wind. Too much wind, however, will blow the pollen too far away, while rain simply washes it away. The farmers keep a very anxious eye on the weather at this time of the year.

Approximately four months after flowering, the grapes should be ready to pick: it is the time for *vendanges*, as the harvesting of the grapes is known. Before this time, however, the grapes must ripen to produce the necessary sugar content to allow for fermentation – the more sugar the merrier, up to a point. August is the month when the most heat is needed – "*Août fait le goût*" (August brings the taste to the grape), say the farmers. They live in constant fear that the weather will let them down at this crucial time.

The life of a *vigneron* is certainly all Champagne, but most definitely *not* all bubbling fun. The Champenois work long and hard to bring their vines to the peak of productivity, but their task has only just begun when the grapes have ripened. The *vendanges* marks the beginning of a second cycle of intensive work.

Hautvillers

The abbey of Hautvillers was once one of the most powerful political and religious institutions in Champagne. It was also where the famous Dom Pérignon worked as cellar master, contributing so much to the development of the area's prestigious sparkling wine.

Hautvillers was founded in 650 AD and soon became a pilgrim centre and one of the most powerful and revered of all the French monasteries. For almost 12 centuries it was a recognized place of rest for pilgrims from Northern Europe en route to worship at the shrine of Santiago de Compostella in Spain. Its monks were famed especially for their beautifully illuminated manuscripts.

During its lifetime, the abbey has seen a fair amount of action. By 1562, it had been burnt down four times, and yet it had still survived as a monastery. The leaders of the French Revolution, however, abolished monasteries and sold off their lands, so Hautvillers ceased to exist as a religious institution after 1790. The abbey was looted by Russian troops in 1814, and Jean-Remy Moët's son-in-law, Comte Pierre-Gabriel Chandon, bought what was left, leaving the church to the village's care and building himself a new *château* in the abbey grounds. In 1870, the estates were requisitioned by the Prussians; in the First World War it was used by the Italians and then the allied forces of England and France. The Chandon *château* was burnt to the ground in the Second World War, and its gardens were devoted to vegetable production for the duration. A detachment of the British RAF Air Service was stationed at the abbey at the beginning of the war, and attacks from the German bombers were frequent. The building managed to survive these onslaughts, but when the German occupation began, it was more or less abandoned and fell into a state of disrepair.

In 1960, for the first time in 200 years, a religious group established itself at Hautvillers. A dozen or so Carmelite nuns used it as a centre for nursing and other works. These sisters eventually moved elsewhere, and Monsieur Jean Couten, chairman of Mercier and mayor of Hautvillers, took control of the property.

Under his direction, Hautvillers and its beautifully restored buildings have been brought back into useful life.

Hautvillers today

The abbey is now a museum of Champagne, and a Foundation for the exchange of intellectual ideas. The director of the Foundation is Monsieur Pierre Emmanuel – poet, writer and member of the *Academie Française*. Monsieur Jean Couten, who has now added a directorship of the Moët-Hennessy group to his many distinctions, is manager of the abbey. He is trying to extend its appeal to attract modern students and interested visitors. The abbey is not only a museum of wine history, it is also a "shrine" to the sacred memory of Dom Pérignon.

Couten sees himself as something of a detective in his endeavours to reconstruct the atmosphere in the abbey as it would have been in the Middle Ages, when the first Benedictine monks were living and working there. He has also gone to great lengths to represent the environment in which the famous Dom himself worked during the reign of Louis XIV. The original wine presses, casks and viticultural instruments are all on display, in "realistic" settings, and the museum exhibits contemporary letters, books, paintings and other artefacts which explain the life and career of Dom Pérignon. There are other temporary displays featuring historical subjects of particular relevance to the region, such as Napoleon's association with Champagne and its wine.

Under Monsieur Couten's orders, the old abbey vineyards are being replaced with vines that are almost exact duplicates of the kind which flourished in the 18th century. The same grapes are now growing on the same land, and being cultivated by the same methods, as in Dom Pérignon's day. Monsieur Couten believes that in a few years, Hautvillers will be able to produce Champagne that is a perfect copy of the original Pérignon wine.

The abbey of Hautvillers, home of Dom Pérignon from 1668 to 1715 and today a museum of the Champagne industry.

Making the Wine

Between being picked and being pressed, the grapes have hardly time to draw breath, for their juice has to be turned into must (unfermented grape juice) as soon as possible. The successful production of clear white wine relies on the briefest possible contact between the skins and the grape flesh, since the skins colour the juice. Contact with the skin of either black *or* white grapes causes the juice to darken. In the case of black grapes, the juice starts almost immediately to turn red. When you are trying to make the clearest and most transparent of sparkling wines from black grapes, as in Champagne's case, the slightest blush is anathema.

Almost as soon as they have been picked, the grapes are taken off to the winery for pressing. Speed is of the essence, since prolonged contact between the grapes' flesh and their skins results in discoloured must.

An expert touch

Subtlety is what the Champenois are proud to claim as their advantage over the pressing methods practised by all other wine producers. Champagne grapes are pressed so delicately that their skins are hardly even broken. The juice, or must, of both white and black grapes is expressed, but the skins are only folded. This has the additional advantage of keeping the seeds, and their unwanted bitter flavour, inside the skins, and allows their juice to run down into the gutters of the press, having had practically no contact with the skins. The CIVC's rule is that the maximum load for a traditional Champagne wine press cannot be over 4000kg (8800lbs) of grapes, producing about 2666l (586gal) of must, or 100l (22pt) of must for every 150kg (330lbs) of grapes.

The selective process

By law, the extraction of the must is carefully rationed in four quality categories. The first 2050l (451gal) pressed is known as the *cuvée*. This must will have obviously more freshness and *finesse* than the must that comes from the second and third sequences of pressing – the *tailles*.

The *tailles* are handled in two sections, the *première taille* and the *deuxième taille*, producing a total of 616l (136gal) of must. The *cuvée* and the *tailles* together are the only parts of the juice that is allowed to be used for *appellation* Champagne wine. There is still juice in the grapes, even after

The courtyard of the Pommery winery in Bouzy at the turn of the century. The baskets loaded with grapes were tended carefully by the *vignerons* en route from vineyard to press house to minimize the risk of damage.

these pressings, so they are pressed for a fourth time, in what is known as the *rebêche*, to producing juice that cannot be used to make Champagne. This juice goes to make table wine, or is distilled to make brandy. The squashed grape skins are used as animal fodder, or as fertilizing mulch in the vineyards.

The mechanics of pressing

The Champagne presses are wide and flat compared to those of other varieties of wine. To keep the juice from any unnecessary contact with the crushed skins, the presses are only 75cm (29½in) deep, so that the juice from the top layer of grapes can only run that far through the other skins. Presses may be either square or round. The parts that touch the grapes are of oak.

Whether round or square, the part of the press that holds the load of grapes resembles a big baby playpen, slatted like a picket fence. The round type is more efficient, since it spreads the pressure more evenly over the whole area. Vintners are beginning to show a marked preference for round presses over square. A lid, reinforced with metal bars and hinged to allow for easy opening and cleaning, is forced down vertically into the "playpen" by hydraulic or electric power. Vertical presses are still considered to give the best quality juice, even though they were invented 200 years ago. Champagne is experimenting cautiously with new press ideas. Methods such as the inflatable bag, and the helical (screw-type), allowed since 1971, are being tried out, but the old timers still believe that the ancient way gives the best quality must.

Pressing has to be done quickly as the ripe grapes pour in from the gatherings of the *vendange*. Pressing 4000kg (8800lbs) of grapes takes about four hours. But the press gangs eat and sleep beside their work for 10 days or more.

Pressing methods have changed very little over the years. Applying pressure on the grapes vertically is still considered the most efficient method of extracting the best quality juice.

Cleanliness is not only next to Godliness; in the wine-making industry it is essential, if the vintner hopes to keep his wines sound. Before and after the harvest, the winery is given a thorough cleansing. The presses are inspected and tested to ensure that they can stand up to the 10 solid days of work they will have to do.

The must is left for half a day in airtight tanks to allow impurities (bits of leaf, twigs, dirt from the vineyards) to settle. The juice that might have been pinkish in colour on arrival in the tank becomes straw-coloured after it has been left to sit for 10 hours. Then the juices begin to vinify, and the vintner must take things in hand as soon as he can.

The first fermentation

Turning grape juice into Champagne wine is a double process. The vintner oversees two separate fermenting periods. In the first, the natural yeast enzymes break down the sugar in the grapes to convert it into alcohol and carbonic acid gas (carbon dioxide). This may sound unpleasant, but in fact you find carbonic acid gas in almost any "charged" water.

Sometimes, in cold climates like that of Champagne, the grapes do not enjoy enough sunshine to make the necessary 17g of sugar per litre they require to produce each one per cent of the natural alcohol that will turn the grape juice into wine. A finished still wine will contain from 8 to 14 per cent alcohol. In Champagne's case, the alcoholic content is usually between 10 and 11 per cent.

If the sugar content is not high enough in the must produced, a procedure called "chaptalization" is allowed. This means adding enough sugar to augment the natural grape sugars and stimulate the production of the desired amount of alcohol. The process was named for a Monsieur Jean Chaptal who was Napoleon's Minister of the Interior for five years, from 1800. It was he who first made this treatment legal in cooler climates where it may be necessary to promote the alcoholic content of a wine.

Storing the developing wine

In the famous *méthode champenoise*, the first fermentation, encouraged in 99 per cent of the Champagne makers' proceedings by chaptalization, takes place in huge tanks, or *cuves*. These days, the *cuves* are made of stainless steel. Some are vast tanks made of cement lined with fibre glass or ceramic, or polyester. Their filling and emptying is "handled" automatically from a central panel of computers.

A few of the most traditional houses still use ancient oaken casks. Oak gives the wine a more "old-fashioned", subtly smooth flavour. Although both methods are equally effective as far as quality is concerned, wines vinified in wooden *cuves* have ardent fans. There is no doubt that the wines produced in this way taste different. They are also more expensive to make because a big oaken cask is less easy to keep in good condition than its stainless steel counterpart. Such a *cuve* is also liable to lose up to a bottle's worth of wine every month, through evaporation.

A wine cellar full of modern *cuves* is an impressive sight. Each tank can hold 30–50,000l (6,600–11,000gal) of fermenting wine. The splendour of a 30m (100ft) row of these monsters, with their tremendous, shimmering, stainless steel heights and the smooth shiny curves of their bodies, can transform a simple warehouse into an awe-inspiring Champagne "cathedral".

Some Champagne Houses vinify all their wines in spotless new stainless steel *cuveries*. One such House, Charles Heidsieck, employs a system whereby each of its 154 huge individual vats is assigned to the wine from a particular vineyard. Thus the firm can vinify its wines according to the individual character of the different vineyards. The vats were made to their cellar master's exact specifications.

The first fermentation of the Champagne process takes place in enormous *cuves*, tanks or casks. Most Champagne producers today use stainless steel tanks (*right*) for practicality and because they do not want the natural flavour of their wine to be affected by the seasoned wood of the old-fashioned casks (*below*).

The elements of change

As soon as fermentation stops, nitrogen gas is introduced into the vats to cover and thereby protect the must from contact with air, which would oxidize it. Making good modern wine has a great deal to do with controlling temperatures. While it is fermenting, a process that entails a sort of friction between carbon dioxide and oxygen that generates heat, the wine must not be allowed to reach a temperature of over 22°C (72°F) and the heating must take place slowly and smoothly. Modern fermenting tanks control the heat by means of a cooling waterfall that slides slickly down the sides of the tanks.

Carbon dioxide can be dangerous in large doses, so the enclosures in which today's tanks stand are well ventilated and often out of doors, sometimes open to the sky. In days gone by, the oaken casks for fermenting were kept at ground level for maximum coolness. But because the gas is heavier than air and sinks rather than rises, the cellar floors became very dangerous places to work. It was not uncommon for workmen in the old enclosed fermenting rooms to keel over in a faint from an increasing lack of oxygen.

The early part of the first fermentation, which lasts for about 10 days, makes the must seem to "boil". Yeast enzymes consume the sugar in the juice, converting it into alcohol by means of violent chemical processes. After 10 days, the "boiling" dies down, but the fermentation goes on for another couple of weeks. The yeasts themselves, having done their work, gradually die, leaving very little sugar in the wine – only about 2g per litre. As they die, their remains drop to the bottom of the storage tanks.

The end of the beginning

The must from the first pressing of the grapes, (the *vin de cuvée*, the best part), is easier to handle than that of the *tailles*, because it contains more acid, which helps to slow down the rate of fermentation. The *vin de cuvée* is also much less susceptible to diseases and chemical changes than the *tailles* are. When fermentation is over, the wine's temperature is lowered. This is achieved by refrigeration in modern plants, but in the past the cold outside air was simply allowed into the fermenting areas.

Then the wines are "racked". This means they are siphoned or pumped off into other tanks. In former times, they were allowed to flow by gravity from higher barrels to lower ones. This procedure is intended to rid the wine of the debris left by the dying and dead yeasts.

In most Champagne Houses, producers submit their wines to an intermediate, malo-lactic fermentation – a natural process that used to occur haphazardly when, in the Spring, winter temperatures gave way to milder weather. Malic acid gives a certain hard freshness to youthful wine, which softens with age. Lactic acid is weaker and helps to reduce the wine's acidity. Thus a malo-lactic fermentation can be used to alter the flavour of a wine, giving it more depth, if this is considered to be desirable. Scientists can now encourage this fermentation by creating the optimum conditions in which it occurs.

The right blend

After the first fermentation, (and possibly a malo-lactic one), the producer will keep the wines from different types of grape separated from each other. The wine is racked again, twice, to remove impurities. The cellar master, (*chef de cave*), who is often the owner of his own business, and has lived with his wines for years, then begins to prepare for the blending, or *assemblage*, of his latest crops of wines from several different vineyards. His aim is to obtain his own "house style", to give the colour, taste and aroma that he wants to his newly finished wine. The regulations allow him to store up to 80 per cent of his wines from previous years for blending with the new wine.

During blending he will try to keep as near as possible to the same quality, in his new wine, as that to which his customers have been accustomed in the past. But, at the same time, he wants to try to improve on both quality and flavour, if he can, and produce a unique personalized *cuvée*.

The *chef de cave* needs, above all, a good taste memory, a fine "nose" for aromas, and a good colour sense. He needs to understand the nuances of taste, smell and colour, to have years of experience and plenty of intuition. Blending is terribly important to the success of his business, for on his decision depends the possibility of

gaining more customers, merely keeping those he has, or at worst losing them. The burden of responsibility resting on this man's shoulders is enormous.

The importance of the role played by the *chef de cave* is most clearly demonstrated when the grape harvest is poor. Back in 1972, the wines over most of France had a very bad year. Champagne's wines were not good either, but by blending the new wine with excellent wines from 1970 and 1971, they were able to bring the new 1972 wine up to standard. In this way, Champagne can almost guarantee a continuously high level of quality in its top wines. The result is, in effect, an altogether new wine, not merely an improvement on a bad one. Of course, the biggest houses, with a far wider selection of vineyards and stored wines to choose from, have an advantage, under unfavourable circumstances, over those whose choice of wines for blending is by necessity limited.

Crystal clear
Because customers demand perfect clarity in a wine, the blend decided upon is "fined" by the cellar master. A neutral substance, usually a fish-glue, gelatine, or a type of aluminium clay, Bentonite, is introduced into the wine. Any small lingering "foreign bodies" will attach themselves to this so

The *assemblage*, or blending, of the wine is one of the most important stages of the Champagne process. The subtlety and harmony of the blend created by the oeneologists determines the final quality of the wine.

that it, together with the unwanted particles, can be removed easily. The fined and blended wine is given a final racking – sometimes in huge vats holding up to 100,000l (22,000gal) – and is stored in smaller vats until it is needed for bottling.

Containing the sparkle
The next important step is to get the wine into bottles and ensure that a second fermentation takes place. This bottle fermentation is what stimulates the production of Champagne's famous natural sparkle, or its *prise de mousse*. Champagne bottles are made of heavy, thick glass and are strong enough to withstand the 6kg (13¼lbs) of pressure that the wine's carbon dioxide gas builds up inside them – about the same pressure as that you put into your car tyres.

Before the start of the 20th century, bottles had been of uncertain strengths. Champagne's famed cellars resounded with the crack of bursting bottles, reminiscent of wartime fusillades. The danger was severe enough to prompt the producers to furnish visitors with wire masks like those worn by fencers, to protect their faces and eyes from flying glass when they were touring the underground cellars.

Most Champagne bottles today are usually dark green. They weigh a little over twice the weight of their contents. In their bottoms they have a deep indentation, called a "punt" – a vestige from the old days of glass-making, when the punt indicated the point at which the metal rod, used to hold the molten glass, was broken away. In Champagne, this indentation is used for one-handed pouring of the wine – by putting the thumb into the punt and spreading the fingers across the outside of the bottle as you pour – a procedure that never fails to impress guests. The punts are also useful when stacking bottles upside

down once they have been cleared of their sediment. The cork of the upper bottle fits comfortably in the punt of the one below. In this way up to 30 bottles can be stacked, one above the other, to save space in the crowded cellars.

A Champagne bottle holds 75cl (1⅓pt) of wine. For special occasions, the largest bottles easily available today are double magnums, (the equivalent of four bottles each), called Jeroboams. Although they are no longer made, there do exist huge containers, shaped like Champagne bottles, called Nebuchadnessars, holding the equivalent of 20 bottles of "bubbly", and needing at least two men to pour out their contents. Unfortunately, these "special" bottles are not as much of a treat as they seem. The wine inside them has had to be transferred from its original bottle and in transit will have lost some of its sparkle.

Champagne bottles receive their first temporary cork and are left *sur lattes et sur lies (right)* until fermentation is complete. Although Champagne is only fermented within standard or magnum size bottles, it is sold in a variety of different volumes. From left to right: Rehoboam — triple magnum; Jeroboam — double magnum; magnum; bottle; Imperial pint (now obsolete); pint; quarter or nip.

From cask to bottle

After blending the wine is transported to the bottling line – a long, noisy, clanking battery of machines. These can automatically handle the various processes of filling and capping.

The first of these is called the *tirage*. The maker adds to the wine the *liqueur de tirage*, which consists of a little *cuvée* wine mixed with sugar, and a quantity of yeast – a *liqueur* very different from those you might serve after dinner! The sugar is attacked by the yeast and their interaction produces the in-bottle sparkle that is the hallmark of the *méthode champenoise*. The quantity needed depends on how much gas pressure the particular House wants in its wine. 4g of sugar, for instance, will produce one atmosphere of pressure when the temperature is 10°C (50°F), giving the producer a Champagne containing 10 per cent alcohol.

Champagne usually ends up containing about 6 atmospheres of pressure, as a result of the addition of 24g of sugar. Since most of the sugar is converted into alcohol during fermentation, the amount of sugar added **relates** solely to the amount of "fizz" a maker wants his wine to have. The maker also selects the yeast he feels will ferment well at low temperatures and leave lees that will settle easily within the wine.

The *liqueur* is carefully measured into each bottle by automatic equipment which turns the bottles upside down and shakes them to be sure the mixture is evenly distributed through the wine. The bottle is then automatically corked, and trundled off to the immense cellars to lie in state on its side, *sur lattes*, (*lattes* are the laths that are placed between the layers of bottles), for a legal minimum of one year for ordinary Champagne, and three years for vintage. However, the best makers keep their wines *sur lattes, et sur lies*, (*lies* are the deposits of dead yeast cells within the bottles), for three years for ordinary, and five years or more for vintage.

The first cork

These days the first corking is done with a metal "crown cork" to make future operations easier to handle. Before being "crowned", a plastic, cuplike plug, like a small top hat, is placed in the bottle neck.

Its purpose is to contain the *lies* and therefore make them easier to remove before the bottle gets its final cork, in a process known as *dégorgement*. Some Houses still use a real cork for the period of rest because they believe that the wines age better behind this type of cork, but high costs have forced the majority of them to switch to crowns.

An underground transformation

Champagne's bottles do not only rest and age in the perfect conditions of its vast cellars; they are transformed there, becoming sparkling, developing their bouquet and improving their "bio-chemical" qualities. Unlike the carbon dioxide produced in the first fermentation, which evaporates into thin air, the gas from the milder second fermentation is imprisoned in the wine, inside its bottle. This is the *prise de mousse* that makes the wine effervescent. The longer its undisturbed cellar life is, the smaller and more lasting its bubbles will be on opening. The wine actually "ripens" inside its container. Houses that have *crayères* like to age all their wines in them. The temperature is perfect: a constant 9°C (49°F). For this reason, some producers say that the *prise de mousse* is more effective in *crayères* than in ordinary cellars.

The wine stays in the bottle along with the "bones" of the new yeast that has been judiciously added. The wine and these natural lees remain together until the Champagne is old enough to be sent out into the Great Wide World on its own. While *sur les lies*, the wine becomes re-enriched with some of the nitrogen that the yeast had used up during fermentation and it gains an extra aromatic quality.

A final purification

Despite all the racking, filtering, fining and other clearing procedures that have been done, there are still many dead yeast cells suspended in the wine which need to be filtered. During its three to five years rest, these tiny impurities fall to the side of the bottle, forming a clear line of deposit that must be eliminated.

They undergo another special handling process called riddling (*remuage*) to get rid of this sediment once and for all. The bottles that have aged sufficiently are taken

from the impressive ranks of resting Champagne bottles to be riddled in one of two ways. Hand *remuage* is still kept up for some of the top quality wines, more for the sake of tradition than for practicality, or because it gives better results than machine riddling. This method is, of course, also very interesting for tourists to watch. The bottles are contained in holes, bored at an angle of 45° through a thick wooden board to create a special rack. They are initially laid in the holes almost horizontally, with a slight tilt from punt to neck, but as they are riddled they are gradually raised up until they are more or less standing on their heads. The lingering sediment will have been shifted down into the plastic "cup" in the neck of the bottle where it can be easily removed. The *remueurs* themselves probably end up each day with a permanent nervous twitch in their overworked arms and hands – just like Charlie Chaplin in the film "Modern Times"!

The modern method involves stacking the bottles in special palettes that are set into *remuage* machines – called *gyro-palettes*. A *remuage* machine looks very much like a Second World War rocket launcher. It is essentially a metal frame that holds the palettes into which the bottles are slotted horizontally. In the larger Houses there can be as many as 60 of these

Dégorgement by hand is rarely undertaken nowadays. The efficient modern machinery that inserts the final cork and *dosage* as the temporary one is removed has superseded this highly skilled but unreliable method.

"launchers". 504 bottles are placed in a riddling machine at one time. The apparatus jiggles them all at once; then it shifts them 40° to the left or right. The palettes are simultaneously tilted so that the bottoms of the bottles are raised by about 1cm (½in) with each jiggle. After several days the machine will have tilted all the bottles in the palettes to an inverted position ready for *dégorgement* to take place.

Today, one man can handle from 40 to 50,000 bottles in the time it used to take to hand-riddle approximately 6000. But it is not only the increased production speed that makes machine *remuage* preferable nowadays. According to Michel Budin of Perrier-Jouët, using the mechanized riddlers saves a great deal of storage space. It is possible to riddle 1–2000 bottles per square metre mechanically; whereas by hand, only about 80 bottles can be riddled in the same space. So time and space are saved without having to settle for an inferior end result.

The final stages

After *remuage*, the bottles are re-stacked, this time upside down, with the cork of the upper bottles firmly nestled in the punts of the lower ones. They are left in this position until they are taken to be disgorged, a process also mainly done by machine nowadays.

The bottles are placed, still inverted, in smaller palettes. These palettes are then moved to a large tank of freezing salt water and the necks of the bottles are thrust into the icy brine. The sudden reduction of temperature solidifies the wine behind the temporary cork, and in the plastic cup, into a sort of slush. The crown cork, (and the plastic cupful of debris), is mechanically and rapidly removed. It shoots out of the bottle neck, propelled by the force of the carbon dioxide gas.

At this point things become frantic, even though the process is fully automated. The bottle is given a tiny squirt of *dosage*, or *liqueur d'expédition* before the final cork is

The traditional method of hand *remuage*, supposedly introduced by Madame Clicquot in the early 19th century, is still used by many producers today. Some, however, prefer to use machines, which have been developed to do the job equally well and more quickly.

bunged rapidly in to prevent any loss of liquid (the frozen wine prevents the escape of carbon dioxide for just long enough), and the bottle clatters off with thousands of its companions, to be dressed in its glamorous shipping finery.

The *dosage* is a dash of sweetness that determines whether the product is to become a regular *brut*, or one of the less popular *extra-sec, demi-sec* or *sec* types. Less than 15g of *dosage* added per litre of wine permits a producer to call his wine *brut* – the grade preferred nowadays by the majority of consumers. Between 12–20g of sugar produces an *extra sec*; 17–35g produces *sec*; and 33–50g produces *demi-sec*. Different markets like different levels of sweetness. Some prefer non-dosed wines that are as dry as a bone – *brut zéro, brut sauvage, ultra brut*, or *brut non-dosage* – but these are still in the minority.

Corking up

The neck-freezing method has been used since 1889, but it has been mechanized to a sophisticated level in recent years. At the end of the 19th century, *dégorgement* was undertaken entirely by hand. A man would hold the bottle between his knees and knock out the temporary cork by loosening the *agrafe* – a metal clamp holding it in place. The gas, plus a slight nudge from the workman, would push the cork out. Then the race was on for the *dosage* and the new cork to be added as fast as humanly possible. The *dégorgeurs* had to be very quick and skilful, and a great deal of Champagne must have been lost when they were learning their trade.

In the modern method, the final cork is forced into the bottle by the same machine that removed the old one and added the *dosage*. The cork is usually laminated. Before insertion it is a fat, very light, compressible bark cylinder, at least twice as wide in circumference as it is when it has been in a bottle for a long time. The section of the cork that is forced into the neck of the bottle is of course compressed, but the rest of it remains in its original form and gives the Champagne cork its classic mushroom shape. A metal cap is immediately place over the head of the "mushroom" and is wired to the bottle to prevent the gas, (or rough handling), dislodging the cork. A cork that reveals a

bell-shaped end when drawn indicates a relatively young wine. A cork drawn from a bottle of well aged Champagne will have a slender, pencil-like stem.

The shape of luxury

The bottle is finished off with its golden foil cork-cover, its label and any other decoration particular to its House. These can be severely *distingué* or rather garish, incorporating stars and red "diplomatic" sashes. All the labelling and decoration is done by machine, except in the case of some of the extra-special *cuvées*, vintages and gift packs. Some producers are putting their best vintage into very handsome bottles, decorated with painted flowers or specially commissioned designs that are baked on to the glass. As the French author, Guy Magnin puts it: "Even before it is poured, Champagne impresses us with its splendid garments, enhanced as they are with silver and gold."

When the bottles of Champagne have been disgorged and the *liqueur d'expédition* added, the final cork is swifly forced into the bottle against the force of the escaping gas pressure. Nowadays, corking is executed in a rather more sophisticated way than it was in the early days (*below*).

78

The
Finishing
Touches

These 19th century etchings depict the process of Champagne bottling at Pierry. Although the sequence of activities at this stage of production has not changed since the beginning of the Champagne industry, both the producers' capacity and the speed of all the processes have altered dramatically. This is, of course, largely due to the substitution of traditional skills, such as those illustrated here, with mechanized methods. The almost domestic atmosphere of this packing house has been replaced with one of well-oiled efficiency, the disgorging and bottling machines employed to maximize the rate of production and to minimize wastage.

The disgorger

Corking

Fastening the cork with string

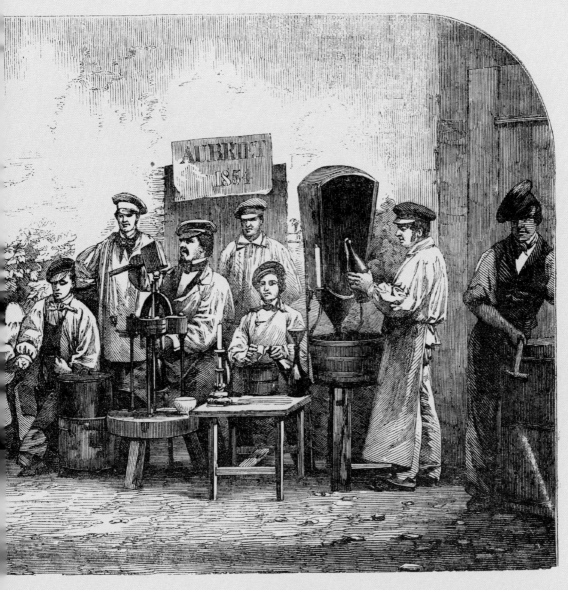

Fastening the cork with wire

Putting on the tinfoil

Wrapping the bottle in paper

The Champagne Houses

"Champagne is like music. It has to be identified by name. You don't say 'I've listened to music'; you say 'I've listened to Beethoven, Mozart, or Berlioz.' It's the same with Champagne. You need to know who is behind a label."

This is the opinion of Rémi Krug, one of the Champagne men whose product is part of the texture of Champagne's renown throughout the world, and it is shared, I believe, by most of his colleagues. The following collection of brief portraits of some of the best known Houses in no way implies any judgement of their respective standings. They are all highly respected and produce much appreciated brands of the best that Champagne has to offer.

The Jardin Anglais at the beautiful Maison Moët & Chandon in Epernay, which echoes the pair of guest pavilions that Jean-Remy Moët had built in the style of the Trianon Palace at Versailles, in honour of the Emperor Napoleon.

Ayala & Cie

Although Ayala has its headquarters in the town of Ay, its name has nothing to do with the town. The firm was founded by the son of a Colombian diplomat who was posted in Paris, Edmond de Ayala. The young Edmond fell in love with and married the niece of the Vicomte de Mareuil, who owned the Château d'Ay. The Ay vineyards were her dowry and the couple set up the company simply as a logical result of their happy union.

Today Ayala makes about 900,000 bottles of wine a year. Its Champagne is traditional in style, fruity and of a high quality. Ayala belongs to the amorphous group of Houses known as the *Grandes Marques*. Its present chairman, Jean-Michel Ducellier, took over from the distinguished René Chayoux in 1968. He has been president of the *Union des Syndicats de Champagne*, and co-president of the CIVC.

Under his directorship, Ayala has diversified a little, becoming the owner of Château La Lagune, a fine high quality Medoc. It is still very much a family affair, however. Its cellars are housed at the splendid 18th century Château de Mareuil, 3km (2mi) outside Ay. Its three old vertical presses and the old *cuves*, which also date from the 18th century, are to be found at the Château. Its working presses and both a wooden *cuve* and a glass-lined one are kept in Ay itself. Monsieur Ducelier himself takes charge of the final *assemblage* after the numerous tastings that are involved in the blending. The Ayala blend is generally made from 70 per cent black grapes and 30 per cent white, all from top ranked vineyards. Twenty per cent come from Ayala's own 99 per cent rated vines.

Ayala's non-vintage *brut* is kept *sur lies* for two and a half years, its vintage *brut* for six months longer. Until recently, Ayala also produced a *blanc de blancs* vintage, which served as the House's special *cuvée*. A new special *cuvée* was launched in 1987. Its "Brut Rosé" is particularly successful in export markets.

Ayala in fact exports about half of its production. Its main market is Great Britain, which buys about 140,000 bottles a year. Germany and Belgium follow close behind the British lead. Ayala is hoping to develop a market in the Far East and thereby raise its export total to 65 per cent.

Bollinger

"There is never a limit to quality," says Christian Bizot, the Président-Directeur-Général (or "PDG" to use the French abbreviation) of Bollinger. He has been in charge of this distinguished family firm since 1978, a year after the death of his aunt, Madame Lily Bollinger, the post-war *Grande Dame* of Champagne.

Madame Bollinger was one of the great personalities in Champagne's history. She ran her firm for 35 years in a very personal

Madame Lily Bollinger, the redoubtable widow who ran her family firm for 35 years. During the Second World War when petrol was scarce, she could often be seen cycling energetically through the countryside inspecting her vineyards.

way. During the Second World War, when there was a shortage of petrol, she could often be seen inspecting her property on her bicycle, keeping a close watch on the progress of her grapes. She has left ample evidence of her enthusiasm for her wines: "I drink Champagne when I'm happy, when I'm sad, sometimes when I am alone. I trifle with it when I'm not hungry, drink it when I am. When I have company I consider it obligatory. Otherwise, I never touch it – except when I'm thirsty!"

Bollinger's quality has been of the highest since time immemorial, and this peak of excellence is maintained using traditional methods. "We still ferment our must in small wooden kegs," says Bizot. "And we age our wines behind real cork. We keep most of our reserve wine in glass magnums, because we believe that the perfection of our blend merits the expense. We have a stock of reserve wines significantly larger than that of most Houses."

Bollinger always keeps its precious stock of reserve wine for at least five years before using it in blending. Some of the wines used in their R.D, *Récemment Dégorgée*, vintages have been lying on their lees for over a decade, allowing the wines to develop fully their individual aromas and tastes. Bollinger's meticulous production process follows Bizot's maxim: "Speed is the enemy of quality."

Seventy per cent of the grapes they use come from their own vineyards. Six of them, in Ay, Bouzy, Louvois and Verzenay, are rated at 100 per cent; the rest average 98 per cent. Bollinger's vineyards extend across 57ha (140 acres), 49ha (120 acres) of which are in production.

Bollinger produces full-bodied wines using Pinot Noir and Chardonnay grapes, adjusting (or, as Bizot would say, perfecting) the flavour with a small percentage of reserve wine to achieve the distinctive House "personality". Monsieur Bizot has confidence in the appeal of his wine: "James Bond likes it, and so do Prince Charles and Prince Andrew apparently, since both of them served Bollinger at their weddings!" For the Prince of Wales it was a "Bollinger R.D, Vintage 1973." For Prince Andrew, it was one that the Palace "just happened to have in their cellars" – a vintage 1966.

Many Champagnes have tended to become lighter in style since the end of the Second World War, claims Bizot, simply because the officially sanctioned area of vineyards has doubled, and although perfectly acceptable and legal, these areas produce less "weighty" grapes. Bollinger prides itself on not using any grapes from these new zones.

Bizot is not at all worried about future supplies of grapes, or the challenge of new competitors. "There can be no shortage of grapes when cheap Champagne is available, so people's fears must be unfounded. All the really good land is already in the hands of people who are established growers or producers. The fact that prices for new land are high, combined with people's unwillingness to sell, makes it almost impossible for new producers to enter the market and upset the trading balance that exists today."

Veuve Clicquot-Ponsardin

La Veuve Clicquot, or the Yellow Widow as she became known from the unusual label she designed for her non-vintage wine, was one of the most successful of the Champagne widows. It was her determination that kept the firm running after her husband's death, when her father-in-law put it into liquidation. Her success was due partly to her optimistic attitude and unremitting dedication, but mostly to the committed work of her enterprising and efficient chief salesman, the German, Monsieur Bohn.

His approach to promoting the Clicquot product was very different from hers. For example, during Napoleon's final struggle to save his Empire, the Russian soldiers occupying Reims took to drinking the bottles of Champagne which they had looted from the Clicquot cellars. Madame Clicquot shrugged off the loss. "Let them drink," she said. "They will pay later." And she was right. It is certain that Monsieur Bohn would not have reacted with the same equanimity. In 1814, he was sent to Russia with a shipload of Clicquot Champagne. "I shall make it known," he said, "that the whole consignment has already been sold, and that only if I am offered an enormous price will I consider parting with a bottle. How cruel and severe I am going to be!"

He was a shrewd and persuasive salesman. On the same Russian trip, he was waiting for a visa at Koenigsberg, when he decided that he could probably do some business there. "I don't ask anyone to commit themselves to an order," he wrote to Madame Clicquot. "I just distribute the address of my hotel and I receive more visitors than I would have believed possible! All I am doing is educating people." He was perhaps unusual among salesman in his genuine belief in his product. "Your wine is nectar," he wrote to his employer. "It has the power of Hungarian wine [Champagne tended to be sweet in those days] and the colour of yellow gold. There is not a trace of cloudiness and the *mousse* is such that when the cork is released, half the contents of the bottle hits the ceiling!"

By the time he reached St. Petersburg on October 15th, he had pre-sold most of his cargo at 12 roubles a bottle. "My goodness, what a price! What good news! I am overcome with joy – no waste at all". By the time he left Russia, he had sold 30,000 bottles and claimed that he "could have sold 20 or 30,000 more".

One of Clicquot's main claims to fame is probably the fact that it was the House responsible for perfecting the system for ridding the wine of its yeast deposits – *remuage*. Madame Clicquot and her cellar master invented the wooden *pupitres* into which the bottles are slotted for riddling. The *remuage* methods they employed are still used today, though many Houses are switching to mechanical methods that can do the job both quickly and just as efficiently, (see p.75).

Veuve Clicquot today owns 265ha (644 acres) of high quality vineyard and is the third largest landowner in Champagne. These vines provide a quarter of the firm's requirements and the additional grapes are bought from the many small holders whose equally good vineyards surround the Clicquot property. Over 35 different *crus* can go into a final blend for each vintage. As is the case with all Champagnes, the wine that is created from the blending is of a far higher quality than its components. Clicquot's fame was founded on its Yellow Label non-vintage *brut*, but it also produces a "Gold Label Vintage", a vintage *rosé*, (Clicquot claims it was the "inventor" of *rosé* Champagne), a rich, sweet *demi-sec*, and its prestige wine "La Grande Dame", which is aged for six years.

The former Clicquot mansion on the Rue du Temple in Reims, is preserved more or less as it was in the Widow's day. It is a very lovely house in which the company entertains its guests in high style – complete with butlers and all. The guests of Yvan de Navacelles, Clicquot's director of Public Relations, gather in the charming living room, or dine under the benign gaze of the Widow, whose famous portrait by Léon Cogniet hangs on the wall of the dining salon.

Co-opérative de l'Union Champagne

The industrial and agricultural co-operative movement originated in England with the Rochdale Society in 1844, although some years earlier, the French had established producers' and consumers' co-operative societies. In Champagne, the co-operative idea developed with a vengeance only after the Second World War. In the Champagne industry, a co-operative, (or co-op), is usually an association of growers who are too small to cope with their own vinification or storage, and who therefore join together to share the necessary facilities. A co-op may also act as a sales and marketing office for its members. It is allowed to sell its wines, but not to buy other wines and re-sell them. A co-op provides a measure of security for the small growers, and by so doing it helps to maintain the stability of the region's economy. A monopoly on the sales of Champagne by the larger Houses would not be economically healthy, and the various co-ops enable the smaller producers to compete and maintain the trading equilibrium. However, should a co-op become strong enough to threaten the position of the big Houses, it would cause unrest, but the rigid traditional structure of the Champagne industry means that the likelihood of this happening is remote.

There are several sorts of co-operative in Champagne: those that deal with the pressing and vinification of the grapes, those responsible for the marketing of the wines, and those who buy the agricultural equipment and supplies for their members. In all the co-ops have around 10,000 members. There are about 145 growers co-operatives, 130 pressing and vinification co-operatives and 15 marketing co-operatives.

The director of the Co-opérative de l'Union Champagne, Monsieur Henri Geoffroy, used to be the head of the Champagne Growers' Association. His organization is vast, uniting about 10 smaller co-operatives to help them with vinification and marketing, providing everything from helicopters to spray the vines with sulphate, to machinery for riddling, not to mention the all-important business advice. The Union is based in a very modern office in Avize, a village on the western edge of the Côte des Blancs, complete with huge picture windows, and extensive cellars and bottling lines.

The Union serves about 14,000 vineyard owners, who are themselves members of smaller co-ops, based mainly in the Côte des Blancs. By selling their wines through the co-op, they can do as well financially as they might by selling to the large Champagne Houses. The Union has contracts with various Houses which commit them to buying 60 per cent of its produce, all of which is sold in *cuves*, not bottles. The oeneologists of the purchasing House control the blending of the co-op's *cuvée* with their own wines to produce the blend they require. An *assemblage* or blend of only *grand cru* is not necessarily the best, in Monsieur Geoffroy's opinion: "It is a scaffolding on which to build or blend a better wine." This blending of different wines from different sources is a perfectly normal procedure and has been the accepted practice in Champagne for many years. The Union is special in the fact that its wines come from only the top quality vineyards and that it deals with only the best Houses.

Each *cuve* is identified by its origin and the grapes it contains. The co-op wine that is not bought by the Houses is given back to the producers to sell – sometimes under their own labels. About 10 per cent of the Union's total production, (about 1,200,000 bottles), is sold to Marks and Spencer's retail wine shops in Great Britain. Another good customer is the Orient Express company, which supplies Union Champagne on the famous train journey between London, Venice and Istanbul. The Union also has its own brand, "Saint Gall", but Monsieur Geoffroy admits that it is not an aggressive sales organization.

Deutz & Geldermann

"Our philosophy is simple," says André Lallier, owner and chairman of this small but prestigious House. "It is to limit our sales efforts to connoisseurs, three-star restaurants and specialist stores." Lallier, a tall, distinguished gentleman and a member of the fifth generation to run this family business, is conservative and dedicated to quality, but he is not adverse to progress and has begun to diversify.

"There are not enough grapes in Champagne for everyone," explained Lallier's young sales manager, Christophe

Hubert, "so we have invested in the Côtes du Rhone red wines, in whisky, and we have started to cultivate vines in California's Arroyo Grande in Santa Barbara state. We also have interests in both red and white wines in Australia and Argentina." The firm has also exported its expertise as far afield as Korea.

The House was founded in 1838, and it still operates from the town of Ay as it did then. It owns some 40ha (99 acres) of vineyards in *grand cru* areas, which provide the firm with 40 per cent of their grape requirement each harvest. They undertake all their vinification using traditional methods. The *remuage* is done by hand, there is no fining or filtering and the second fermentation takes place in magnums or Jeroboams. The Deutz operation in California will follow the traditional principle of minimum mechanization, although fermentation will be done in stainless steel *cuves*. "We went into this enterprise with C & B Vintage Cellars – the subsidiary of Wine World – who will sell both the French and American wines," explains Monsieur Hubert. Deutz's total production only amounts to 800,000 bottles a year. About half is exported, with 70,000 going to the USA, and 50,000 going to West Germany.

In spite of the firm's traditional production methods, Monsieur Lallier has not hesitated to support modern art. His recently disgorged vintage *cuvée*, "Georges Mathieu", is decorated in a startlingly radical style. Its cork and neck are encased in a white "cloak", with the word "Deutz" scrawled flamboyantly across it in an artistic hand. The label covering the lower quarter of the bottle is half orange and half white, again with the word "Deutz" printed on it. The effect is striking to say the least. Georges Mathieu designed the label to be "resolutely modern".

The Deutz family home is right next door to the winery. It is a perfect example of Third Empire interior design and is maintained in its original condition – dark wood panelling, mohair furniture, contemporary paintings, aspidistras and all! The winery premises are in fact behind the house, on the hill at the back of Ay. The vineyards extend beyond them. The entire complex of buildings gives the impression of having been whisked unchanged from the

19th century to this and life seems to go on pretty much as quietly as it ever did in this *quartier* of Ay.

Charles Heidsieck

Although it is the youngest of the three Heidsieck firms, Charles Heidsieck is second in line in terms of sales with a total annual production of about three and a half million bottles. The firm was founded in 1851 by Charles-Camille Heidsieck, and ever since, the male members of the family have been given hyphenated names – one of which is always Charles. It must be very confusing at family reunions! In 1985, Charles Heidsieck became part of the Cognac group of Rémy Martin and Krug.

The managing director of the new organization is an energetic Hollander, Gijsbert Hooft-Graafland, who began his career in the cigarette business, until Moët-Hennessy wooed him into the wine trade.

Charles-Camille Heidsieck, the firm's eccentric founder, was fêted all over the world as "Champagne Charlie" in music and comic song.

The classic *pupitres*, in which the bottles of Champagne are placed to be riddled, dwarfed by the majestic vaults of Charles Heidsieck's shining *crayères*.

He was poached from Moët by Charles Heidsieck where he is very content to stay. "My first priority", he says, "is to keep the wine at its natural best. Great Champagne comes from good grapes and good handling. We cannot improve on Nature; but we can maintain it at its best. We know how to make wine; which slopes are the most productive; how to prune properly; that it is best to keep to a certain level of picking per hectare – and so on. Our skill must be to interfere as little as possible."

Charles Heidsieck uses up to 40 per cent reserve wine to give its blends smoothness and flavour. All its wines are vinified in stainless steel tanks, of which there are 154, so that the produce from each vineyard can be treated separately. The wines are aged in what I believe are the most beautiful *crayères* in the region. Shiningly white, they have a true sense of mystery and the past and you half expect to discover druids, or magic wines, or Merlin himself when you visit them. They have been left almost exactly in their original condition, except for the levelling of their floors, since the Romans abandoned them in the first century AD. They can only be visited by appointment, because Charles Heidsieck is concerned that they should be preserved in mint condition.

The firm first became widely known through the reputation of its founder Charles-Camille. He made his first sales trip to America in 1857, where he was almost immediately nick-named "Champagne Charlie" because of his flamboyance. During the Civil War, he decided to cross the Confederate lines so that he could collect a few debts in New Orleans. He disguised his aim by taking the trip dressed

as a barman on a Mississippi river boat, but
at the same time he was smuggling a
"diplomatic bag" through the lines for the
French Consul. Unfortunately, the Yankees
had captured the city by the time "Charlie"
arrived there, and he languished as a war
prisoner in a Mississippi military fort for
four months! When he was freed, he blithely
continued to sell more and more of his
Champagne. Later Heidsiecks have
extended the firm's export market to
include the Far East, South America and
Australia.

"People like Champagne because it is
light and tastes marvellous," says Monsieur
Hooft-Graafland, "although, unfortunately,
effect rather than taste is often their
criterion when judging it. We try to keep
abreast of the new technology so that we
can continue to improve the quality of our
product." Charles Heidsieck's non-vintage
"Brut" is its best seller, with its elegant nose
and light golden colour. Its "Blanc de
Blancs" made entirely from Chardonnay
grapes, is powerful vintage perfection and
sells mainly to restaurants. Its "Brut
Sauvage Vintage" is made with 75 per cent
Pinot grapes and 25 per cent Chardonnay.
Its "Rosé" is light and agreeably soft, while
"Champagne Charlie", its prestige vintage
is a fresh and cheerful wine.

Piper-Heidsieck

The present chairman of Piper-Heidsieck is
François, the Marquis d'Aulan, son of the
Marquis de Suarez d'Aulan, and a direct
descendant of Florens-Louis Heidsieck. His
father, in 1942, turned part of the Piper
cellars into a clandestine arms depot for the
French *Résistance*. The Germans got wind
of the hideaway and sent to arrest him, but
the Marquis managed to escape to Spain
and then to Algeria, 10 minutes before they
arrived to pick him up. Later, he joined the
Lafayette Squadron and was shot down
while on a mission and killed at Mulhouse,
not far from Champagne. The young
Fréderic Heidsieck, an enthusiastic skier,
serves today as his family company's export
manager. "It takes 200 years for a House to
become a *Grand Marque*," he says, and he
should know – the firm has been among
this élite group for that long.

Piper is currently involved, in co-
operation with the CIVC and the other
Grandes Marques, in experiments to find

less expensive and more efficient ways to
turn grapes into Champagne. "None of the
modern techniques being used in
Champagne today make direct contact with
the wine itself, thus guaranteeing its natural
character", explains Fréderic. "*Remuage* by
machine does not involve contact with the
liquid. *Dégorgement* using little cups to
catch the sediment on the cork, and
freezing the top of the bottle neck to make
the removal of that cup and its contents
easier, do not touch the wine either. We
are working on two techniques which may
remove the need for *remuage* altogether."

One of these techniques involves the use
of *bulles*, little porous gelatin capsules,
containing yeast, which allow the wine to
filter through but prevent any yeast from
escaping into it. The other uses a yeast that
is packed in tight clusters, or agglomerated.
In both, there is no yeast sediment left in
the wine. The pellets of yeast will drop on
to the cork in a contained form, making it
easier and quicker to eliminate the spent
cells, instead of having to wait for them to
drift down through the wine. The time
spent riddling today – up to three weeks –
will be saved. The experiments are expected
to continue for at least two more years.
"We, the producers, are perfectly willing to
accept new methods, as long as we can be
certain that they work! But we also want to
maintain tradition and preserve the mystery
of Champagne," says Fréderic.

Piper makes several special *cuvées*. One of
them, the "Rare 1976" is now a classic
vintage wine. It is made exclusively from
the excellent 1976 vintage *cru*, using the
hand-picked grapes from only top quality
vineyards and the must from the first and
lightest pressing. Another great wine is the
vintage "Brut Sauvage", which has no
added *dosage* and is made using 90 per cent
Pinot Noir and 10 per cent Chardonnay.
The high percentage of the Pinot Noir
compensates for the lack of sugar and gives
the wine a naturally balanced flavour. The
firm is fond of using magnums to present its
wines, because "they are more impressive
and more convenient for use at a big
gathering. One bottle will serve as many as
eight or 10 people."

Piper also produces a *rosé* Champagne,
but it is treated with some disdain by young
Monsieur Heidsieck: "It is different; it has
snob value and is popular mostly in export

markets." However, he is well aware of the importance of export sales. Piper has come to realise that the export market could well be more secure than the domestic. This is partly because smaller growers in France are increasingly selling their wines under their own labels, and are less and less willing to sell to the big Houses. The competition on the home front is phenomenal.

Like many other Champagne Houses, Piper-Heidsieck has begun to expand its business. It is now the chief shareholder of an estate, called Piper-Sonoma, in California, where it has established a branch of its wine industry. Piper sells over 100,000 bottles of Champagne in the USA, half a million in Great Britain, 300,000 in Italy, and 200,000 in Belgium and Germany. Their total sales average about four million a year.

Krug & Cie
The original Champagne Krug was Johan-Joseph, formerly a citizen of Mainz in Germany. He joined the Champagne firm of Jacquesson & Fils in 1841 and married Jacquesson's English sister-in-law. Rather ungratefully, he left 18 months later, to establish his own firm. His son Paul produced 10 children. Joseph II, the eldest, took over the Krug firm in 1910, but sadly he was wounded in the War and it was his wife, as manager, who produced one of Krug's outstanding vintages in 1915.

Joseph II's son, Paul II, was too young to help his mother and ailing father, so a nephew, Jean Seydoux, was called in to help. Paul II eventually took charge in 1959, but Seydoux continued as his respected adviser until his death in 1962.

Paul had close ties with Cognac's Rémy Martin House, which acquired a controlling interest in Krug in 1979. He retired in 1977 and his two sons, Henri and Rémi, now run the company, ably assisted by the widowed Madame Catherine Seydoux. The Krugs are the only Protestant family among the well-known Champagne Houses.

The first bottle of Champagne produced by the Krugs when their House was founded was, according to Madame Seydoux, a "bomb", a sensation, because it was so different from other Champagnes – it was not sweet! Krug, she says, remains different in both taste and style. "Krug is first of all a wine – *then* a Champagne." For many wine

The founder of Champagne Krug, Johan-Joseph Krug, learned his trade during his brief career at Jacquesson & Fils, and moved to Reims to establish his own firm in 1843.

enthusiasts it is the best.

In the early days, Krug's main exports were to the USA and Britain. Today, over 70 per cent of Krug's output goes abroad – a higher export percentage than that of most Houses. Surprisingly enough, its number one market is Italian. Rémi Krug, a great traveller, was once on a visit to Italy when he came across a farmer lunching on a thick ham sandwich. Beside him no canteen for liquid refreshment was to be seen – only a bottle of Krug! "Now *he* knew how to enjoy life," says Rémi.

Krug's style depends first on its grapes. "We are the only House that makes prestige wines alone," claims Rémi, "Krug is the Rolls Royce of Champagne – there is only one model." The firm does not buy grapes from the south or the west, but exclusively from the heart of the Montagne de Reims and the Côte des Blancs, where it can select grapes from the best of the micro-climates. It buys three quarters of its total grape requirement from growers in these areas and owns the vineyards that produce the rest. Krug has been buying grapes from the Simon family in Ambonnay for five generations.

Krug likes its Pinot Noir to be from south-facing slopes, and its Pinot Meunier from north-facing ones. Chardonnay grapes, "that are totally dry", they buy from *premier cru* vines at Villers-Marmery, in the extreme east of the Montagne de Reims. These "arid" grapes make up part of Krug's distinctive family style. They claim to use only the *cuvée* part of the pressing, never the *tailles*.

Krug is one of the more traditional Houses. Since 1893, the House has kept the same presses. The Krugs and their employees live adjacent to their offices and the winery. The cellars are only two blocks away. "We are not being traditional just to impress the tourists," explains Rémi. "We use the old methods and equipment when we think them good for our wine. When we are 'modern' and 'efficient', it is because we feel it is the better way. We use crown corks, for instance, because there is then no risk of a 'corky' taste, and because they are more practical than the old temporary corks. But we use traditional wooden kegs for vinification because they make it easier for us to blend our wines to our own specific taste."

The wines are kept *sur lies* for at least five or six years. By the time they are sold they are already on their way to the marvellous depth and complexity for which Krug wines are famed. "To hell with making money," says Rémi. "We are not interested in 'average' wine. We like old wines, and ours will keep for up to 50 years if properly stored".

Occasionally the Krugs may keep track of the progress of the wine in a cask by sticking their finger into it, but the serious tasting is done by Paul, (who is clearly only semi-retired), Henri and Rémi. The final blending of a *cuvée* is Henri's responsibility. Krug's reserve wines were stored in magnums until 1962, when steel tanks for the purpose were finally perfected. The company has the capacity to store more than 12 years' worth of reserve wine for use in blending.

Krug's celebrated vintage "Clos de Mesnil" appears only very occasionally. It is made from grapes grown in one small vineyard in the village of le Mesnil-sur-Oger in the Côte des Blancs.

Krug's wines are "hand made – blended with our hearts not just with science. Not one Krug in five generations has ever studied oenology, although we do employ wine experts. The family feeling for wine is inherited," says Rémi. "Champagne is no gift from the gods. It is a human work of art. You impress your own character or taste on your wines. Our basic wines are not astonishingly good, but the blends we make from those wines are *great!*"

Krug sells only some 500,000 bottles of their Champagne a year. Its main brands are "Grand Cuvée", blended from up to seven different vintage wines; "Krug Vintage", made from the grapes of a single, particularly good year; "Krug Rosé", the first *rosé* ever marketed by Krug, brought out in 1983; and "Krug Clos de Mesnil", which is an occasional vintage from a small vineyard that exists today in exactly the same state as it did in 1698. Old Champagne vintages, produced from stocks at least 12-years-old, are bottled and numbered to delight lovers of ancient wines. Rémi says "The *cuvée* is my favourite because it is *mine*. For the vintage, I have to share the credit with God!" He claims that the USA and Britain are vintage maniacs, even though the vintages are not necessarily the best wines.

Lanson Père & Fils

One of the oldest of Champagne's Houses, founded in 1760, Lanson is now owned by one of France's largest food companies, BSN (Bouvois, Souchon and Neuvesel). It is still run by the Lanson family, however, in the person of Maurice Lanson, the nephew of Henri Lanson, who was its director after the Second World War. The Lansons are a prolific and robust family. Maurice is part of the fifth generation of the original farming family which took the firm over in the early 19th century. There is little chance of the family dying out in the near future either: Maurice has 10 brothers and sisters and some 26 or 27 nephews and nieces!

"Making Champagne requires control," says Maurice, "and the CIVC is the perfect mediator. The parallel organizations in Bordeaux and Alsace, CIVB and CIVA, are not so good – we like our CIVC!" The CIVC alone, however, cannot guarantee a good blend; it is up to the producers to regulate their harvest within the confines of

CHAMPAGNE
Laurent Perrier
Cuvée
GRAND SIÈCLE
75cl
TOURS-SUR-MARNE PRÈS REIMS
PRODUCE OF FRANCE
NM 3048262

*Relais et Châteaux 30*ème *anniversaire 1954 - 1984*

The prestigious wines of Laurent Perrier, such as its "Cuvée Grand Siècle," have established it firmly as one of the major *Grand Marque* Houses in Champagne.

official legislation. "Good Champagne must be a light wine, which means that the grapes must not over-ripen. We keep a close watch on the amount of sunshine they get, and hope for a dry summer each year. We were terribly restricted during the two World Wars, but we managed to produce good Champagne nevertheless." Lanson's careful viniculture is obviously very effective.

The firm has seen its fair share of history at first hand. During the last war, there were several American army camps surrounding Reims, which were named for American towns such as Boston, Cleveland and New York. Army public relations advisers took local children to visit these camps, and they in turn were duly taken on tours of the Champagne cellars. The Armistice was signed near the Lanson offices, and the temporary residence of General Eisenhower, who was made an honourary citizen of Reims, was opposite them. Nobody knew when or where the Armistice was to be signed, but the day before, Maurice's father came into the office and said: "Something important must be happening! There's a German car parked outside our offices!" The actual room in which the Armistice was signed was in a school several blocks away. It is probably one of the ugliest famous historical monuments in the world.

Like most of the Champagne Houses, Lanson is beginning to diversify. It has set up a marketing organization for Port wine; Scotch, Irish and malt whisky; gin; as well as for its own "bubbly". The flagship of Lanson's output is its "Black Label" non-vintage. It also produces a more expensive *rosé*, a still Bouzy red wine, and a white Chardonnay Champagne. A small quantity of Ratafia liqueur, and a Marc brandy, made from the crushed grape skins, are produced. Its prestige wine is called "Noble Cuvée de Lanson". Its stocks of wine total 20 million bottles, plus a further 12 million bottles of reserve wine for blending. The House sells about five million bottles of Champagne every year.

Veuve Laurent Perrier & Cie

Laurent Perrier, which now sells a phenomenal seven and a half million bottles of Champagne a year, conducts its business from a building on the site of what was once a flourishing 11th century abbey in a tiny, isolated village on the banks of the Marne, near Ay. The company's business dominates the village and the surrounding countryside, where four of its vineyards, rated at 100 per cent, are situated. It is incredible to think that Laurent Perrier's huge international reputation stems from such a tiny village, but perhaps it is just proof of the maxim that quality always outshines quantity.

The famous Champagne widow whose name the company has retained, ran the business for 38 years, between 1887 and 1925, but she failed to maintain it profitably and died without heirs. Just before the Second World War, it had dropped from its position among the top 10 Houses to be ranked at only 100 and it was on the verge of bankruptcy. Fortunately, the name of Laurent Perrier was saved from ruin when the company was taken over by Marie Louise de Nonancourt, the sister of Victor and Henri Lanson. The Lanson family kept the company running under its original name and restored it to international prestige.

Madame de Nonancourt was widowed during the war and the business was placed in the capable hands of Henri Gondry, her director general. Her son, Bernard, is now president of Laurent Perrier. He took over control in 1949 from Henri Gondry, who personally undertook to educate him in the wine business when Bernard returned from his perilous wartime experiences working with the *maquis*. During Bernard's presidency, the House has gone from strength to strength and today is among the top six Champagne producers and a member of the *Grandes Marques*. It is one of the few surviving independent family-owned firms in Champagne.

The Laurent Perrier plant today is ultra-modern, by contrast with the ancient ecclesiastical buildings that house it. The firm uses stainless steel storage tanks. "Wine from *inox* [stainless steel] is perhaps no better than from oak, but its quality is certainly more reliable," says Emmanuel de la Giraudière, Laurent Perrier's able export manager. "So our installations are still expanding." More buildings are under construction to enable the company to cope with its annual output. Its new caves will allow the firm to store as many as 11 million bottles. Surprisingly enough, in spite of these moves towards greater modernization, Laurent Perrier still does most of its *remuage* by hand.

The company, like its competitors, prides itself on the exclusivity of its top wines. Only five per cent of its total production is used to make its famous "Grand Siècle". Both Emmanuel de la Giraudière and Bernard de Nonancourt are firm believers in the fact that Champagne is a unique beverage that should be treated with some reverence. The production process is meticulously controlled. "Champagne is a hand-crafted product and should remain so," says Monsieur de Nonancourt.

This dedication to Champagne does not prevent Laurent Perrier from expanding its horizons beyond the confines of its home territory. The company has joined together with the American firm, Almaden, and now produces a "Laurent Perrier Blancs de Blancs" sparkling wine from grapes grown in southern California, of which it is also justly proud.

The years of austerity, suffered by all Champagne producers during both World Wars and the Depression of the Thirties, are definitely over for Laurent Perrier. They own about 80ha (197 acres) of vineyards, and they own more uncultivated land which can be developed if necessary. Their land is classified as being of a quality averaging 90 per cent. The company's prosperity was demonstrated recently at its lavish 175th anniversary celebration. Monsieur de Nonancourt took the entire staff of Laurent Perrier and their families, (350 people in all), on a three-day cruise around the Mediterranean on the steamship Danaë. His guests were also treated to an enormous birthday cake and, (of course!), several bottles of Laurent Perrier.

Moët & Chandon

It is hard to keep track of the various changes undergone by this company, the largest Champagne producer in the world, since its humble beginnings. The founder of Moët & Chandon, Claude Moët, had been a wine broker and salesman, but in 1743, he

began a career as a wine producer. Working with his son, he created a flourishing wine company to pass on to his grandson, Jean-Remy. The young Jean-Remy sold his Champagne to the military school at Brienne, where Napoleon was then a student. The two men became friends, and this special relationship brought Moët fame and fortune when Napoleon became Emperor of France.

Jean-Remy was elected mayor of Epernay, and as such it was his official duty to entertain the Emperor as he passed through Champagne on his frequent military campaigns. Jean-Remy had an imitation of Louis XIV's famous Trianon palace at Versailles built in Napoleon's honour on the Avenue de Champagne in Epernay, where he could entertain his Imperial guest in style. These meticulous duplicate buildings stand opposite Moët's main offices and are still used today as guest houses for visiting VIPs.

Napoleon made Jean-Remy a member of the Legion of Honour just before his defeat and temporary incarceration on the island of Elba. During the Congress of Vienna, the heads of all the nations involved in creating a peace treaty stayed at Moët's guest pavilion in Epernay. In true political style, neither the guests nor their host were in the least inconvenienced by Jean-Remy's sudden change of loyalty. In fact, the firm seems not to have been affected at all by the swift alterations in the French government that occurred during Napoleon's decline. Wellington and Blücher descended on Monsieur Moët to enjoy his hospitality after Waterloo, and Charles X, the new King of France, graced the second Trianon with his presence too.

On Jean-Remy's retirement his son, Victor, and his son-in-law, Pierre-Gabriel Chandon, took the firm over and changed its name to Moët & Chandon. Under this new partnership, the House went from strength to strength and achieved particular success on the French market. Moët was also the brand leader in Great Britain and in many other countries worldwide, producing some two and a half million bottles yearly. Even in the early days, the company owned more vineyards than any other Champagne House – covering 360ha (889 acres) around top quality villages in the Montagne de Reims, Vallée de la Marne

and Côte des Blancs areas. Today, Moët's buildings extend through a large part of Epernay, with miles of cellarage stretching underneath them, and the company owns about 500ha (1235 acres) of vineyards – still the largest holding in the region. It buys its additional wines from certain co-operatives, (see p.87) it knows and trusts. The House blends its *cuvées* in consultation with the chosen co-op and its own wine experts.

One of Moët & Chandon's most important assets is their monopoly on the name of Dom Pérignon, the legendary

One of the earliest bottles of Moët Champagne, together with a pair of traditional flute-shaped glasses. Today, Moët & Chandon's extensive cellars at Epernay house thousands of bottles, very different in shape and volume (*below*).

"inventor" of Champagne. Their vintage "Dom Pérignon" is widely held to be the most exquisite Champagne available. Its bottle and label are exact replicas of the 18th century bottles which make up part of the firm's collection of memorabilia. This homage to the great Dom is considered a fitting tribute to the man who made Champagne what it is today.

"Secondary fermentation was just a nuisance to the makers of Champagne's early still wines," explained one of Moët's wine experts. "Dom Pérignon took advantage of this 'aberration' and experimented with it to make sparkling Champagne. He didn't 'invent' Champagne, but he brought improvements to the way grapes were handled. For example, he invented the method for slow, gentle pressing in wide shallow presses that prevents the grape juice from staying in contact with the grape skins for too long. He realised that the caked, pressed skins are very thin and that if the dripping juice runs through them quickly, it will not get stained." Dom Pérignon's skilful experiments blending different types of grapes to produce a *cuvée* of blended grape juices is considered at Moët to be "the secret and strength of Champagne today."

The man who has had an immense effect on Champagne's fortunes in recent years has been Comte Robert-Jean de Vogüé, one of the region's most farsighted and energetic figures. He was president of Moët for 40 years and was the moving spirit behind the establishment of the CIVC and worked within it, as a secret member of the *Résistance*, to frustrate the German occupying forces in the area, (see p.47). His clandestine activities were eventually discovered and he was sent to a concentration camp.

He survived the ordeal and returned to Moët & Chandon to build it into Champagne's largest firm. It is due to his imaginative conception of what a Champagne market could be that Moët has continued to expand. It was at de Vogüé's instigation, that Moët bought Ruinart in 1963, the perfume house of Dior in 1968, and Mercier in 1970, and that it merged with the Hennessy company in 1971. This conglomeration is today one of the largest luxury goods suppliers in the world.

The three Moët-Hennessy Champagne

Moët & Chandon wines have been popular with many different clients over the years. Napoleon I was a friend of Jean-Remy Moët, seen (*right*) welcoming the Emperor to the Maison Moët & Chandon, and, together with his wife Josephine and many other important statesmen, a regular customer.

Houses retain their individuality as far as their different markets are concerned. The sales areas for each brand are defined by its personality and traditional image, so that there is no internal competition. Moët & Chandon concentrate mainly on the export market; Mercier is strongest in the domestic market; and Ruinart deals with private customers, connoisseurs and its own exclusive export clientele.

According to Moët-Hennessy's Champagne and Wines manager, Yves Benard, the group is staffed mainly by Champenois, since it was Robert de Vogüé who created it, Benard, like all his colleagues, makes his decisions independently as a local man who knows his Champagne, but he must include the requirements of both the subsidiary Houses in his organization of the buying of grapes, equipment, and bottles, and of the shipping. In 1986, the group sold a total of 24,000,000 bottles – more than double what they sold 10 years ago. Vinification,

blending, *dégorgement*, bottling and all such operations are undertaken separately by each House. Labelling and shipping, however, are organized from the Moët-Hennessy centre in Epernay, situated right on the railway line. The system is run as efficiently and as cost-effectively as possible.

Moët was the first Champagne to be quoted on the French *bourse*, or stock market, and the company has been the leader in promoting the production of sparkling wines around the world. The company once owned cellars in Luxembourg and in Trier, Germany, where "Chandon Mousseux" and "Chandon Sekt" respectively were produced. Today, "Chandon Sekt" holds the top position in the German market. Moët was also the first company to produce an American sparkling wine – "Domaine Chandon" – in the Napa Valley, California.

Robert de Vogüé's beautiful home at Mareuil-le-Port is not far from Epernay. He indulged his penchant for naturally harmonious exterior decoration by permitting only white animals and birds to wander in the grounds. The effect of the moving white spots over the smooth green grass was delightfully humorous. Monsieur de Vogüé was never without a twinkle in his eye. Another beautiful mansion connected to the Moët company is the Château de Saran, which overlooks sweeping hillsides covered in vines. The company use the Château to entertain clients, wine merchants, writers, and international connoisseurs. The generous hospitality enjoyed by the many different guests, is a masterful promotional ploy that has paid huge dividends over the years.

Mercier

Just before the Second World War, Mercier was the second largest Champagne firm and the one that held the prime position in the French market. It has retained the latter reputation: of its six million annual output, 88 per cent is sold in France, where it is even better known than its big brother Moët. In fact, you can still see 50-year-old metal plaques advertising its product, tacked up on buildings and roadside walls.

Mercier has always been aware of the importance of publicity. Its founder, Eugène Mercier, loved to put on a show and he had his vast Second Empire cellars – which stretch for 18km (11½mi) – magnificently decorated for the delight of visitors. The celebrated Navelet brothers executed a series of carvings in the chalk walls, one of which depicts beautiful dishevelled girls enjoying Champagne from the fashionable *coupes* of the time. Mercier also had a railway line built to bring deliveries and guests into the cellars. Visitors invited to see the *crayères* travelled in an electric train on this railway, as they do to this day, for a dramatic first look at Eugène's flamboyant *cave*. Its features include the huge "Caveau Bacchus", dug out of the clay, where 200 people can sit down to a Champagne dinner. During the Second World War, frivolities such as holding a Ball were forbidden by the occupying forces, but the beleaguered locals discovered the perfect clandestine venue for their parties in the enormous soundproof cavern, where they could dance and sing the night away without fear of interruption from their hated enemies.

Another impressive "gimmick" is a huge, ornately carved oaken cask, which holds the equivalent of 200,000 bottles, situated just inside the entrance to the cellar's "railway station". The same cask was used in 1889 for another publicity stunt that astonished and delighted everyone who witnessed it. The cask was dragged by 24 oxen from Epernay to Paris to take part in the Great Exhibition. To get the huge procession through the towns along the route, Mercier had to tear down buildings, widen roads, and strengthen bridges. When the cask arrived at Paris, the workmen had to widen the existing gateway in the city walls to allow the monstrous creation through.

Eugène was the first Champagne producer to use the new cinema industry to advertise his wines. He employed Louis Lumière, the French inventor of the cinematograph – the first real motion picture projector – to make a publicity film about Mercier. He also set up a variety of publicity stunts. In 1900, at the Universal Exhibition in Paris, Mercier invited visitors to go up in a captive balloon to enjoy a bird's eye view of the Exhibition. The balloon was torn loose from its mooring in a high wind, however, and finally set down its terrified passengers in an Alsatian forest – to the delight of the world's press *and* Eugène Mercier! A more successful flight – that undertaken by Louis Blériot across the English Channel – was sponsored by the House of Mercier too.

Today, Mercier is trying to give its Champagne a "youthful" image and recommends that it should be drunk whenever there is a party. According to Monsieur Couten, the chairman of Mercier and a director of Moët-Hennessy, the company is about to launch its wine in Italy and Spain, but until then its market

will remain solely French as it has always been. Mercier Champagne tends to be mostly *brut* or *demi-sec* and much of it is sold to the "CHR" (*commerce, hôtelliers, restaurants*) trade. Its vines are mainly in the Vallée de la Marne and in the Aube region to the south.

The electric railway leading into the magnificent "Caveau Bacchus" in the Mercier *crayères* (*left*). The enormous ornately carved oaken cask (*below*) holds the equivalent of 200,000 bottles of Champagne and was used in the memorable publicity stunt for the Paris Exhibition in 1889.

Ruinart Père et Fils

According to Bertrand Mure, the chairman
of Ruinart, Père et Fils, "Champagne is the
drink of the gods". His House is the oldest
that operates under its original name, and it
is still among the top *marques*.

It was founded in 1729 by Nicolas
Ruinart, the nephew of the famous monk,
Dom Thierry Ruinart, who had been a
friend and colleague of Dom Pérignon's at
Hautvillers. Nicolas was a linen merchant
by trade, who changed his profession on the
strength of the popularity of his homemade
wines. He had been in the habit of
presenting bottles of his still Champagne to
his best customers, and the enthusiasm with
which they were received persuaded him
that he could make a good living from his
wines alone.

It was Nicolas' son, Claude, who really
put Ruinart on the map, when he moved
the firm's headquarters to Reims from
Epernay and was honoured by Louis XVI
with the title Seigneur de Brimont. It was
during his lifetime that Ruinart began to
use the Roman *crayères* as cellars for storing
their wines at the perfect temperature.
Ruinart was the first House to discover this
ready made storage space. Their *crayères* at
St. Nicaise which spread underground for
8km (5mi), are today classified as being of
particular historical interest and are open to
visitors. They comprise three levels, or
floors, extending to a depth of 30m (100ft).
The reception of the must, blending and
bottling usually take place on the
uppermost level, while the second is where
the bottles are left to age. The third and
lowest level is where the wines are racked,
fined and riddled. Fortunately, a lift has
been installed to carry you back up to the
surface! The *crayères* are very beautiful and
are still kept in the condition in which they
were discovered 250 years ago.

Claude's son, Irinée, took over the family
business on his father's retirement. He
entertained Napoleon on his way back from
his disastrous campaign in Russia, but as
soon as the Emperor was overthrown, Irinée
changed allegiance and became Mayor of
Reims by Royal decree. In 1825, he was the
host of the last king to be crowned at Reims
cathedral, Charles X, who raised him to the
rank of viscount. Irinée retired soon
afterwards and he wrote one of the most
important books on Champagne, the

"Traité sur la Culture en Terre Calcaire".

His son, Edmond, made a perilous sea
voyage across the Atlantic in 1832 to
present President Jackson with a case of
wine and introduce the United States to
Ruinart Champagne. Their "Tête de
Cuvée" is still a very popular brand in
America. Edmond's son, Edgar, travelled in
the opposite direction to sell Ruinart wines
in Poland and Russia. His promotional visit
included a meeting with the Tsar and was
instrumental in establishing the highly
lucrative Champagne market with pre-
Revolutionary Russia.

During the First World War, Ruinart's
offices in Reims were totally wrecked by the
shells fired by "Big Bertha", and André
Ruinart was forced to conduct his firm's
business from the secure *crayères*.
Unfortunately, a shell burst a water main
near this hiding place and the cellar was
flooded. Undeterred, André continued his
work on a raft, floating in this secret
underground lake.

In 1950, Ruinart joined with Baron
Philippe de Rothschild, of Bordeaux's
Château Mouton fame. Since 1960, the
company has been a subsidiary of the huge
Moët-Hennessey-Dior conglomerate,
producing some 1,300,000 bottles of
Champagne yearly, of which 60 per cent is
exported. Ruinart has retained its
prestigious image and operates
independently under Bernard Mure, a
nephew of the Ruinarts.

The majority of its grapes come from the
Côte des Blancs and the Montagne de
Reims. Its best selling brand is the vintage
"Dom Ruinart Blancs de Blancs", made
with Chardonnay grapes from both these
areas – a selection from the villages of
Avize, Cramant and Mesnil, (for delicacy
and subtlety), and from Sillery and Villers-
Marmery, (for body and finish). The end
result is an elegant, exquisitely dry wine.
Another great wine is the vintage "Dom
Ruinart Rosé". Its blended brand is called
"R de Ruinart", and it also produces
a vintage version called "R de Ruinart
Brut Vintage".

Over the years, the list of the firm's
clients has included some surprising and
famous names. The Archbishops of
Canterbury and York bought Ruinart wine
in 1797; the Duke of Marlborough and the
king of Prussia in the same century were

also admirers of their wines. Ruinart's devotees in the 19th century included the Duke of Wellington; King Leopold of Belgium; Napoleon and Josephine, (who reneged on her Champagne bills after her divorce from the Emperor); and the wily French politician, Talleyrand. In recent years, customers such as Brigitte Bardot, Gina Lolobrigida and Sophia Loren have lent Ruinart a touch of glamour, while Edward Heath, Andrei Gromyko and Giscard d'Estang have brought the company political distinction.

G.H. Mumm & Cie

The initials G.H. in Mumm's company name stand for Georges Hermann, whose German father, together with his two brothers and a friend, started the business in 1827. Georges took the firm over in 1853 and for the next 50 years the firm was run by members of the Mumm family, although they never became French citizens. The company's "Cordon Rouge" Champagne, with its distinctive red ribbon, symbolizing the Legion of Honour sash, across its noble chest, was introduced in 1875 by Georges and has become famous in its own right.

During the First World War some of the Mumm family decided to place their allegiance with the Kaiser and their property in Champagne was sequestered. The part of the family that remained in France renamed the company the *Societé Vinicole de Champagne Successeurs*. In a later lawsuit, the entire family was prohibited from ever owning any part of the firm because of the vindictive behaviour displayed throughout the trial.

During the occupation of France in the Second World War, French laws were suspended. One day, a German officer marched into the company's Reims office and announced: "Ich bin Graff von Mumm!" A member of the Mumm family was again able to run the firm – at least for three years!

In 1955, Seagram Distillers, the giant Canadian spirits firm, bought into the company, becoming its major shareholder in 1972. Alain de Gunsburg, the son-in-law of the founder of Seagram, is now chairman of the board, and Mumm has acquired two other Champagne houses – Perrier-Jouët and Heidsieck & Cie. Monopole. The Mumm Group today has interests in Scotch

The Mumm Group, which includes the Houses of Perrier-Jouët and Heidsieck & Cie. Monopole, is the second largest producer and exporter of Champagne. Mumm, like so many Champagne Houses today, has begun to diversify. They now trade in Scotch and Irish whiskey and in Taylor's port.

and Irish whiskey, and in Taylor's port and produces a total of 14,100,000 bottles of Champagne a year, of which over nine million are exported. The Mumm Group is the second largest producer and exporter of Champagne.

"Champagne is to sparkling wine what a sports car is to a mini," says Monsieur Cense, Mumm's export manager. "Real wine connoisseurs enjoy something complex and refined, and that's what a fine Champagne is." But he believes that the modern trend is towards a more neutral wine, lighter and more elegant than the older wines on which Mumm's reputation was founded. The traditional taste was for fruitier, powerfully flavoured wines, and they cater to this today with their "Cuvée René Lalou", which is a prestige vintage wine, presented in a beautiful fluted bottle. "It seems quite sweet, as does any white Champagne made from 50 per cent black grapes, but we prefer to describe its taste as 'round'. A wine made from 100 per cent Pinot Noir would be too heavy and rich, although tasty. Such a *cuvée* is considered undrinkable in the USA, but the wine lovers in the UK seem to enjoy the strong flavour."

Mumm's "more discreet", less effervescent "Crémant de Cramant" non-vintage is made from 66 per cent Pinot Noir and 34 per cent Chardonnay. Once the private beverage of the firm's directors, its name will have to be altered, since *crémant* is now reserved for use by the makers of France's sparkling *mousseux*. Mumm's other celebrated wine is its vintage "Cordon Rosé", which owes its pink flush to the addition of still red wines from Bouzy.

Mumm's major export market is in the USA, which takes nearly two and a half million bottles a year out of its total exports of 6,737,000, but Canada, Switzerland, Germany and Italy are also good markets. The French market alone absorbs nearly three million bottles of Mumm Champagne yearly.

The striking classical façade of the Mumm company's head office in Reims attracts visitors throughout the year. The bold lettering on the parapet is a particularly unusual feature.

Mumm produces a wide range of different Champagne styles. Its famous "Cordon Rouge" with its distinctive red-sashed label (*far right*) is less dry than many non-vintage *bruts* market.

Perrier-Jouët, Epernay

"Good Champagne is not just a pretty fizz – it has to be first and foremost a very good wine!" This is the opinion of Perrier-Jouët's Michel Budin, the independent director of this subsidiary of the Mumm Group, who was its PDG until 1959 when the takeover occurred. "The quality of a wine comes in the first six months of its life", he continues. "The fizz is the easiest part! Of course, the grapes are very important too. They must be of the best. And pressing needs to be undertaken with love and the utmost delicacy."

Perrier-Jouët produces wine in both the Napa Valley, California, and Australia. The methods required to produce "comparative" wines in these warm climates and in Champagne are obviously very different. The warmer temperatures in America and Australia promote a greater sugar content in the grapes, so the must produced there may need to be doctored with tartaric acid. The wines of Champagne

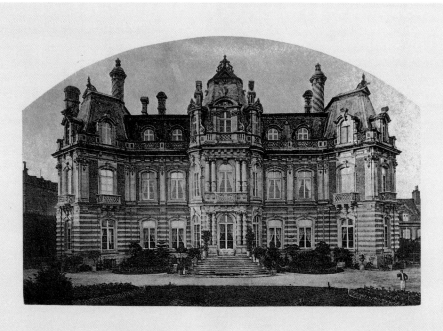

PERRIER-JOUËT & C^{o.'s}
CHAMPAGNE,
ÉPERNAY.

FOURNISSEURS DE SA MAJESTÉ LA REINE D'ANGLETERRE
ET DE SON ALTESSE ROYALE LE PRINCE DE GALLES.

PALE DRY CREAMING
First Quality.
PERRIER-JOUËT & CIE
A EPERNAY.
CHAMPAGNE. DÉPOSÉ.

ENGLAND—INDIA—AMERICA.

never require the addition of acid, but depend on the addition of sugar for a palatable flavour and plenty of fizz. Perrier-Jouët have learnt a good deal from their experiences of wine production abroad.

Monsieur Budin told me, to my surprise, that the dreaded phylloxera louse is still very much alive. No way has yet been found to destroy the killer-bug, so the Champagne growers must still plant American rootstocks in their vineyards if they are to prevent it ruining their crop. However, since the pest lives quite happily on the American roots without destroying them, there seems no reason why the Champagne producers should disagree with Budin's feeling that they can afford to live and let live. In the foreseeable future, grafting will remain a vital part of viticulture in Champagne.

Monsieur Budin is very proud of the present proliferation of Champagne. "Do you realise that the number of bottles we produce in Champagne nowadays [204,000,000] would more than ring the circumference of the earth at the Equator?" Placed cork to punt they would stretch for a phenomenal 50,000km (80,500mi), whereas the earth's circumference is a mere 40,000km (64,350mi). Even Phileas Fogg would have had a hard time getting around that many bottles in 80 days!

Budin has always refused to produce a "Blanc de Blancs" for Perrier-Jouët. He does not see any merit in the practice of using a single type of white grape, year after year, to make Champagne. "A good Champagne needs the balance and depth of red grapes for a really good blend," he claims. "Also, really fine Chardonnays are rare; I don't like using all my best Chardonnays just to make a single cuvée."

But Perrier-Jouët does make special cuvées. It's "Belle Epoque", in its lovely enamelled bottle, is always a vintage and has been a hit ever since it first came out in 1970. The firm's "Blazon de France" is a special, non-vintage prestige cuvée produced when the "Belle Epoque" is not.

The House uses modern riddling

equipment. "Hand remuage", Budin points out, "takes up too much space. You can only riddle 80 bottles per square metre by hand, whereas you can handle as many as 1000 bottles in the same area with machine remuage. So you save space in your cellars which can be used for storage. And machine remuage is just as efficient as the hand method." Someone else I spoke to confirmed this opinion. He explained that a man can only efficiently riddle those bottles that are at the right level for his height. "The top bottles are harder to reach so they get the least attention, and the bottom ones have to be stooped to, so they get none! A machine turns every single bottle the same way and the same number of times, without adversely affecting the quality of its contents."

Perrier-Jouët concentrates on luxury sales. Its wines are a deluxe product designed to appeal to knowledgeable and wealthy customers. The airline "Air France" spoils its first class passengers by serving Perrier-Jouët on its Concorde flights. It sells about a million bottles in France and over a million and a half abroad.

Heidsieck & Cie. Monopole

This branch of the Mumm Group split off from the original Heidsieck company, founded by Florens-Louis Heidsieck in 1785. Florens left the Rhineland and his wool business to become part of the French way of life he so admired. He married a French girl and established his family in France. Heidsieck Monopole was founded in 1834 by the son of one of Florens' nephews. The new firm achieved recognition and success almost immediately, particularly in the German and Russian markets. At one time, the Tsar placed an order for two entire trainloads of Heidsieck Monopole to be delivered every year.

Today its manager, Monsieur Delaître, operates from vast premises in Reims, not far from the headquarters of its parent company Mumm. He is an ardent advocate of more accurate labelling definition. He told me with indignation that in Germany, they used to label "real Champagne as 'Fransoeischer Schaumwein' – French sparkling wine! This practice has been stopped, but some countries still label their own sparkling wines as Champagne." In spite of his disapprobation of these

---

This extravagant Victorian advertisement demonstrates the extent of Perrier-Jouët's appeal in the export — and more particularly the élite — market.

irregularities, he is all in favour of the increasing consumption of sparkling wine worldwide. "It is a good thing that the Americans are starting to enjoy them," he said. "They will graduate from sparkling wines to the real thing eventually!"

He is proud of his House's "Diamant Bleu" prestige vintage *cuvée*, which is sold in a bottle with diamond-like facets cut into its sides. The House non-vintage is "Dry Monopole Brut", made from 100 per cent quality Verzenay grapes, the blackest in the area. It has a fine, fruity nose and is thought to be similar in style to the original *cru* of the region.

Heidsieck Monopole owns one of the most famous landmarks in Champagne – its one and only windmill. Sitting on the peak of a hill at Verzenay, it is used today as a guesthouse and is the company's symbol.

Pol Roger & Cie

Pol Roger's offices occupy a huge museum-like mansion, just off Epernay's imposing Avenue de Champagne, on the sunny north-facing slopes of the town's hillsides. They look out across the valley on to the pleasing vista of their own vineyards.

The company is today run by the great-grandsons of its founder, Pol (the Champenois spelling of "Paul") Roger – Christian de Billy, who handles export sales, and Christian Pol-Roger, who supervises the domestic market. Although the family had their name changed to "Pol-Roger" in 1900, the firm's name remains hyphen-less.

The reception halls of the House's headquarters are full of mementoes of one of its most famous clients, Sir Winston Churchill. Pol Roger has honoured the great man by naming a vintage for him. It produced a "Winston Churchill Cuvée" in 1979, and declared Winston Churchill vintages in 1982 and 1985 for *blancs de blancs* and *rosé* wines. The next Churchill vintage will be put on the market in 1988, while the 1985 will probably not appear until about 1990.

Pol Roger is another of the few Houses

The Heidsieck company promotes its Champagne in this more recent advertisement by exploiting the myth of the wine as an exclusive luxury. Here it is the companion of an obviously wealthy and well-dressed man, substantial cigar in hand.

An attractively stylized advertisement for Heidsieck & Cie. Monopole Champagne depicting a scene of leisurely enjoyment. The ladies are sipping their wine from the wide-lipped glasses fashionable at the time.

that still use hand *remuage*, employing four expert *remueurs*. But the firm has turned "like everyone else" to stainless steel tanks for vinification and storage. "We've had them for 40 years now," says de Billy. "They are unromantic but, we feel, better than wood. Wood imparts a flavour to wine – it's good but it's different. It's a style, like that of Bollinger or Krug. We happen to like our own style".

The firm sells 1,400,000 bottles yearly, of which 60 per cent is exported. "We emphasize quality first, but we do like to expand," says de Billy. Although Pol Roger makes a *rosé* Champagne, de Billy classifies it as "mere snobbery. It is bought in the USA, in England and in Switzerland, but the French don't buy it!" His grandfather, Maurice Pol-Roger, refused to make it, even though Christian assured him that he could sell it easily in South America, where they hoped to increase their market. Later, Maurice reluctantly agreed to its being produced: "All right, make it. But I won't drink it!" In 1959, Pol Roger brought out their first vintage *rosé* – and Maurice never touched it.

Pol Roger owns 75ha (185 acres) of high grade vineyards, which provide them with 40 per cent of their requirements. CIVC regulations have limited the areas of land in Champagne which can be planted with Champagne vines, in spite of the fact that there are certain areas, not included in their classification, which would be perfect for growing grapes. "Locals feel that it would be better to use these fertile areas to grow grapes, than to limit the vines to the poorer soil within the officially regulated

VINTAGE YEAR

Pol Roger is one of the many Champagne Houses that were honoured with Winston Churchill as a client. This cartoon leaves us in no doubt of his predilection for its Champagne! The great man was a frequent guest at the firm's headquarters in Epernay, where many mementoes of his visits are on display.

areas", says de Billy. "But politics and 'democracy' say 'no'."

Their justification for refusing to change the traditionally accepted rules about which vineyard areas may be used for planting is that it would be unfair to both buyers and sellers, and cause more problems than they care to deal with. The value of presently available, authorized land of a lesser quality would plummet, while that of presently forbidden more fertile land would rocket. Thus, at the stroke of a pen, certain presently privileged owners would lose valuable land, while people who now own land that is not designated for plantation would suddenly be able to profit enormously. The upheaval in Champagne would be enormous, so it is generally accepted that such a change will not occur.

De Billy is also sanguine about competition from sparkling wines other than Champagne itself. "People who enjoy bubbles in their wine will always begin to want better ones. Quality is primordial."

Pommery & Greno

In 1858, Madame Louise Pommery, totally inexperienced in both business and the wine trade, went into partnership with

Narcisse Greno, to his great relief. Two years before, her husband had bought into the Greno firm, but unfortunately he had died, leaving his share to his widow. Narcisse Greno was a very quiet man, intimidated by the world of affairs. He retired early on the grounds of being "unwell" when Madame Pommery took over from her husband, but managed to live quite comfortably for 40 years on the proceeds of her success.

Madame Pommery was a very determined lady. She began running the company at the age of 39, with two young children in tow. She made Monsieur Greno agree to two conditions before relieving him of his responsibilities: he had to allow her to start developing sparkling white Champagne, (the Greno company had until then produced only still red wines), and to make a play for the British market. She borrowed money and invested it in vineyards, and in the space of only three years after her husband's death, she had enough Champagne wine – and enough money – to open a London office. During her trips to Great Britain, she met two Scottish lairds, the Duke of Argyll and the Earl of Haddington. She was often a guest at their family homes, at Inverary Castle and Mellerstain in Berwickshire respectively, and their lifestyles impressed her greatly.

She showed her admiration of the Scottish nobility when she built the new headquarters of Pommery & Greno. She bought all 120 of the Roman *crayères* in the Butte St. Nicaise, Reims. She kept 80 to use as wine cellars and sold the other 40 very profitably. Above her cellars, she had huge imitations of her friends' Scottish castles built, so that she could entertain them in the style to which they were accustomed. These castles were not only places of entertainment; they comprised Pommery's offices, the vinification area and all the other necessary working space.

At one time, rumour has it, jealous competitors in Champagne spread the report that Madame Pommery was in financial straits. She quickly thought of a way to discredit their claims. She had recently heard that Millet's famous painting "Les Glaneuses" (The Gleaners), was to be sold to an American and lost to France. She jumped into her carriage and galloped to Paris with 300,000 gold francs to buy the picture herself. With a shrewd sense of public relations she presented it immediately to the Louvre, where it is still on display together with its plaque of thanks from the state. It was obvious to all of France that Madame Pommery was far from poverty stricken.

She was a great patron of the Arts on all fronts. She commissioned the famous Navelet sculptors to carve several decorative bas relief into the sheer white walls of her new *crayères*. These carvings include a depiction of Bacchus, another of Silenus, and a third of a rather boisterous Regency banquet. Recently a new sculptured picture has been unveiled – a portrait of the widow herself by Jean Barrat.

Pommery is one of the biggest landowners in Champagne, with some 307ha (750 acres) of vineyards scattered among over 11 villages. Their equipment is completely up-to-date, including an enormous battery of

stainless steel *cuves* which were installed in 1982 inside one of the "Scottish" castles.

The firm produces four million bottles of Champagne a year and their largest export market is Great Britain. Although it is owned by the enormous French food and beverages purveyors, BSN, (Bouvois, Souchon and Neuvesel), it has retained its distinction. A Pommery Champagne is light and very dry and clean in taste. Pommery has always been a favourite of those who prefer a lighter wine. In Colette's novel "Chéri", one of the characters asks Chéri what she will have to drink. When Chéri asks for Pommery her companion asks: "And before that?" Chéri famously replies: "Pommery before *and* after"! Extravagant but well-applied taste. The *cuvée* is usually made with 60 per cent Chardonnay grapes,

Madame Louise Pommery, who ran the company of Pommery & Greno as successfully for many years after the death of her husband. Her initial inexperience soon gave way to a shrewd and effective business sense.

The incongruous "Scottish" castles
designed and built by Madame Pommery
above her *crayères* in Reims, in imitation
of the homes of her noble friends, the
Duke of Argyll and the Earl of
Haddington.

from Avize and Cramant, and 40 per cent
Pinot Noir, from Ay. *Rosé* Champagnes
make up about 2.5 per cent of their total
annual output.

Louis Roederer

"Give me grapes and I'll make you
Champagne. But give me reserve wines, and
I'll make you Roederer." So speaks Jean-
Claude Rouzeau, grandson of one of
Champagne's most famous widow-owner-
managers: the energetic Madame Camille
Olry-Roederer, who built up her wine's
reputation to its present level and sustained
it for 42 years. That reputation rests on
Roederer's promise that their wines are
blended, using mature reserve wines with
traditional skill, to what they feel is a
perfect standard.

Roederer's pride in its longstanding
tradition, however, does not imply that the
House's approach to Champagne is static.
Roederer has always been an adventurous
firm. Louis Roederer became the owner of a
Champagne House that had been
established since 1776, and he set about

building up the reputation of his wines.
When, in 1870, the Tsar of Russia sent his
sommelier to Champagne to purchase wine
for the Palace of the Kremlin, Roederer
quickly stepped in to corner the Russian
market and persuade the Tsar of the
supremacy of his Champagne.

The regal *sommelier* explained that he
wanted some sort of special packaging on
the Champagne destined for the Emperor.
Roederer came up with the revolutionary
idea of presenting the wine in a clear,
crystal bottle. His son, Louis II, had one
made from true leaded crystal, without the
classic punt in its base. The beautiful new
bottle not only contained the wine safely,
because of its thickness, but became a
symbol of the highest quality Champagne
thereafter. The original crystal bottle is
today too costly to produce, but an
equivalent is made in reinforced glass,
contained in a special paper wrapper to
keep the wine's explosive gas under control.
The "Cristal" Champagne has always been
a vintage dry wine, but two variations are
now produced – a "Grand Vin Sec" with
40ml of *dosage*, and a less dry "Carte
Blanche" with 60ml.

The Russian Revolution of 1917 ended
the Champagne trade with Russia, and
Roederer lost all its Russian stocks. The
firm suffered enormous losses. Russia had
been responsible for 80 per cent of
Roederer's sales worldwide and no payment

was forthcoming for those bottles left in Soviet hands. "We decided there and then that we would never again be dependent on a single market," says Jean-Claude Rouzeau. Nowadays, diversification is seen to be the secret of success.

Rouzeau is a thoroughly modern Champagne maker who is never afraid to branch out in new directions. In 1982, he bought land in Anderson Valley, near Mendocino, California, and planted vineyards there the following year. In one area of this new land, vines were already growing, so Rouzeau simply grafted Chardonnay and Pinot Noir grapevines from France on to these. By 1985, the vines had produced 153t (139 tons) of grapes, and by 1986, a further 214t (194 tons). Roederer is holding the wine from these harvests as reserve wines to blend with its next good harvest. The company hopes to produce its first million bottle *cuvée* of "California Champagne" in 1987 or 1988.

Roederer's vineyards in France encompass 10 different villages, all of which have high quality ratings, averaging 97.5 per cent. The firm therefore has the capacity, within the extent of its own property, to produce an extraordinarily good blend. What little the producers buy to supplement the House's own produce always comes from the same sources, which all average a 95 per cent quality rating.

Roederer traditionally presses its grapes out among the vines. The theory is that this avoids the damage and discolouration of the grapes that can occur during transportation from the vines to the site of the presses. The firm only uses the *cuvée* and the first *tailles* for its best wines, and the must is also decanted in the vineyards so as to disturb it as little as possible. Each plot is provided with a stainless steel storage tank in which to store the must until it is ready to blend and bottle.

Rouzeau himself is a skilled professional oeneologist. Even though he is kept very busy as the firm's director, he plays an important role in creating the ultimate blend of its wines. Roederer does not boast about the individual, personal distinction of its wines' blends without justification. The persistently high calibre of the wines depends on their blending almost more than on the quality of the grapes. The House's all-important stock of *vins de reserve* is

stored in old-fashioned wooden casks, but in modern cellars with inbuilt temperature and humidity regulators. "Reserves are like medicine," says Rouzeau. 'They can be used to 'cure' or improve a wine of weaker quality to bring it up to the high standards we demand."

Taittinger
The Taittinger firm is one of Champagne's most "political" producers. Not only have members of the family made fine wines over the years, they have also been very active in the service of their country, as mayors of Reims and of other towns in the Champagne region, and as senators and deputies of the French Parliament. Pierre-Christian Taittinger was even elected *Président du Conseil Municipal de Paris*, or Mayor of Paris, and was the vice-president of the French Senate.

The Taittingers began their career in the wine industry in 1931, when Pierre Taittinger, Pierre-Christian's father, bought the Champagne company Forest-Fourneaux & Cie. Strangely enough, the Fourneaux family, who established this firm in 1734, also had a political heritage – Nicolas Fourneaux was Conseiller to Louis XV towards the end of the 18th century.

Taittinger's cellars are among the most spectacular of the Roman *crayères*. They were built partly in what was once the crypt of the Abbey of St. Nicaise in Reims. The remains of the crypt are still impressive and the Gothic vaults harmonize perfectly with the mysterious calm of the 2000-year-old chalk pits. The monks who lived at the abbey, when it was a bustling Benedictine centre, traded in wine, and probably used these very same cellars to store and age their produce.

Taittinger's entertainment hall is in a building that once belonged to Count Thibaut IV of Champagne, who is supposed to have brought back the first Chardonnay grapevines from his expedition to Palestine in the 13th century Crusades. Its offices are in the Place St. Nicaise. The Taittinger family home is the Château de la Marquetterie, in Pierry, near Epernay. A handsome 13th century mansion set among Taittinger's own vineyards, it is not without its relevance to Champagne's history. It is said to be where Frère Oudart, a contemporary of Dom Pérignon, experimented with ways of controlling sparkling wine.

Taittinger owns 240ha (593 acres) of vineland and is classed today as a *Grande Marque* House. Its special vintage "Collection" *cuvée* wines are lavishly decorated by artists, such as Vasarelli and Arman, who have painted original designs on gold or silver backgrounds. Its "Cuvée de Prestige" comes in a bottle shaped like a flask, labelled "Comtes de Champagne". It is made only from wines of exceptional years, and with the must from the first pressing of grapes from the Côtes de Blancs.

The firm sells about three and a half million bottles a year. Its main export market is the USA, with Great Britain and Italy coming close behind. Taittinger wines are dry, elegant and delicate.

The Smaller Houses

There are just too many Champagne Houses for me to begin to discuss them all here. In addition to those well-known names I have described, there are a number of smaller, equally prestigious but less famous, Houses, which still produce impeccably made wines. When such a House is blessed with a good vintner; owns or controls a sufficiently wide variety of growing areas to provide fine grapes for blending; and when the weather is favourable, it can produce wines as distinguished as those of the larger Houses. The following is a selection of the best of the smaller Houses.

BESSERAT DE BELLEFON is now a part of the Pernod-Richard company. Its best Champagne is its "Crémant", but it will soon have to change the name of this wine when it can apply officially only to sparkling wines.

BINET FILS & CIE supplies its wine to some prestigious customers, such as Berry Bros. and Rudd wine merchants in London, for example. Its Champagne has a good old-time fruity elegance and a stylish quality.

DE CASTELLANE is the owner of the bulge-topped tower of Epernay and is itself partly owned today by Laurent Perrier. Its wines are light and fresh. The company is very strong on publicity. It began life as the private "toy" of one of Champagne's most flamboyant characters, Louis Boniface Florens, Vicomte de Castellane, "Boni", as he was known, married a wealthy American

and began a life of hedonistic luxury. He threw her an enormous 21st birthday party, with 3000 guests, a 200 piece orchestra, 80,000 lanterns from Venice to light his gardens, 80 dancers, 12 miles of carpeting and several dozen Bengal swans, which he let loose over Paris. When asked why by the Mayor of Neuilly, Boni replied: "Just for pleasure, solely pleasure." He soon went broke, (not surprisingly), but at least he enjoyed himself in the process!

CATTIER is a small producer-grower based at Chigny-les-Roses, on the Montagne de Reims. He owns vines in various mini-climates, so he is able to do on a small scale and less expensively what the big Houses can do: count on fine grapes for his *assemblage*. He makes excellent traditional Champagnes.

GEORGES GOULET is a fine House, linked with Abel Lapitre and De Saint Marceau in *La Societé des Grandes Champagnes de Reims*. It produces rich, full *blanc de blancs* Champagnes.

HENRIOT is now a part of the Rémy Martin company, together with Charles Heidsieck with which it was formerly closely associated. Its Champagne is excellent.

JACQUESSON & FILS was founded in 1798 and still has a very sound reputation.

PHILLIPONAT today belongs to Gosset, the House which claims to be Champagne's oldest, having been founded in 1584. Philliponat produces good value wines and boasts a rare deluxe *cuvée*, made from its single 8ha (20 acre) vineyard, the Clos des Gosses, which has a unique, complex taste. It is produced in limited qualities.

CHAMPAGNE SALON claims to be the first House to have marketed a "Blancs de Blancs". Its wine is a high quality Champagne made traditionally with no refrigeration, not even for disgorging. The company, like Besserat de Bellefon, is now part of the Pernod-Ricard firm. Maxim's of Paris used to serve Salon almost exclusively as its house Champagne

DE VENOGE has been a good, solid non-vintage House for many years. It has recently changed hands and its wines are expected to improve.

An advertisement for Pommery Champagne, depicting a female personification of its glamorous image.

Enjoying the Wine

In the 19th century, the majority of Champagne drinkers in Continental Europe preferred their favourite drink to be sweet. The degree of sweetness or dryness of a wine was entirely in the hands of its maker, who was guided largely by the tastes of the majority of his customers. At the time, one of the most important customers was Russia. This lucrative market had expanded relatively recently. During the Napoleonic Wars very little Champagne reached Russia at all, but what little did was highly appreciated. Madame Clicquot's representative, Monsieur Bohn, who was there in 1810 wrote: "I hear that the Empress is pregnant. What a blessing for us if it is a Prince that she produces! Oceans of Champagne will be drunk in this immense country. Don't mention this at home. All our competitors will want to throw themselves into this northern market." Unfortunately for Veuve Clicquot,

A scene of celebration at the 18th century Russian Court, with a company of dwarves providing the cabaret and serving Champagne. Russia was Champagne's largest export market until the 1917 Revolution.

Napoleon's defeat and disastrous retreat
demolished their hopes of a flourishing
trade, but by the end of the century,
trading revived – especially with the
Russian Imperial Court.

The Russian preference was for very
sweet wines, so the Champagne destined for
St Petersberg would be given a *losage* of up
to 70g per litre. It would seem, however,
that even this level of sweetness was not
high enough for the Russian nobles. They
used to breathe into their glasses of
Champagne until they were clouded with
humidity, and then sprinkle powdered sugar
uniformly around the inside of the glass.
The sugar would dissolve, leaving the
Champagne quite clear, but tasting rather
more like syrup than wine! In Paris, this
Russian habit was imitated in a special
"Romanoff" cocktail, which was a sort of
kir made from Champagne mixed with a
very sweet syrup and served at an icy
Siberian temperature.

From sweet to dry
This vogue for Champagne in the Russian
style was the inevitable result of such a
healthy trading relationship. There was a
glut of sweet wines, produced by the
Champagne houses to compete in this
lucrative market. Gradually, however, the
prevailing tastes in Western Europe
changed, with dry wines reasserting their
popularity over sweet ones. *Les Anglais*,
always partial to dry Champagnes, led the
trend, continually pushing the reluctant
producers to give them dry wines. Since the
English market was not to be sniffed at, the
French were quick to accommodate it,
eventually coming to share as well as cater
for the English taste.

This led to the development of a curious
phenomenon in nomenclature that still
persists today. The Champagne producers
began to describe their wines in terms
deliberately intended to cater to the "dry"
fad, implying that their wines possessed
varying degrees of dryness, even though
they continued to be mainly sweet for years.
Hence the bewildering nominations, still in
use in the 1980s, of *demi-sec* and *sec* for
wines that are, to all intents and purposes,
sweet-tasting.

The sweetness quotient of Champagne
was, (and still is), classified according to
sugar content. A *doux* Champagne is really

**The different Champagne producers
embellish their bottles with a variety of
attractive and eye-catching labels. From
the driest of *bruts* to the richest *doux* and
the most delicate *rosés,* there are flavours
to suit even the most particular
customers. The *brut* and *rosé* wines are
the most popular nowadays, and the
Champagne Houses try to ensure that
they produce enough of both to meet the
demand.**

very sweet indeed, and is very rare nowadays, except for export to the Far East and other specialist markets. *Doux* now contains at least 50g of sugar per litre. The next sweetest wine was named *demi-sec*, in order to cater for those who still liked their dry wine to taste sweet! *Demi-sec* in those days was actually very sweet by modern standards, containing between 33–50g of sugar per litre. *Sec* still contains between 17–35g of sugar per litre, and nowadays, despite the name, is regarded as a reasonably sweet wine. The driest wines were *extra sec* and *brut*, containing 12–20g and less than 15g of sugar per litre respectively.

The modern market

Today, the trend is for even less sugar to be used; some producers are making extremely dry wines indeed. However, it is impossible to do without sugar altogther, since its use is essential to the production of Champagne. Without it, the vital second fermentation could not occur. The *liqueur de tirage* is still usually added, to ensure that this fermentation takes place. These wines are called *nature* or *sauvage* to indicate just how bone-dry they are.

Regulations covering the addition of *dosage* were formalized only fairly recently. Initially, this stage of the Champagne production process was left up to the individual producers and their perception of what the public wanted. Now, the modern producer is required by law to use strictly specific amounts of sugar for each of the recognized types of Champagne, though there is a fair amount of flexibility. The idea behind this is to allow the makers to produce wines with the taste that their customers want, without infringing the legislation. A *brut* for the German market, for instance, may contain 13g of sugar per litre, while another for the British market may contain as little as 2g per litre. The *dosage* is added to the wines automatically, once the level of sweetness has been decided by the cellar master, depending on the particular brand being made.

The alcoholic strength of Champagne is also controlled by law. Non-vintage Champagne must have at least 10 per cent alcohol per litre, while vintage Champagne must have a minimum of 11 per cent. In point of fact however, none of the Champagne that reaches the world markets ever has less than 12 per cent alcohol.

Determining the flavour

Strange as it may seem, the carbonic acid gas produced during the crucial second fermentation also plays an important part in the eventual impact the wine has on the palate. The presence of the gas magnifies and intensifies the sensations that the Champagne provokes in its imbibers. Champagne's sparkle consists of very fine bubbles, suspended like waving threads of beads that rise slowly from the bottom of the glass, or slide up its sides. Their comparative permanence, fineness and slow ascent to the wine's surface is a hallmark of the quality; a frothy "head" on a glass of Champagne is not a mark of distinction.

The perfume of a Champagne, in common with other wines though even more so, depends largely on the grapes used to make it. Chardonnay grapes give the wine a specific and discreet aroma that can be appreciated at its best in a *blanc de blancs* made exclusively from this type of grape. Pinot Noir grapes produce a more mature, "solid" aroma, while Pinot Meunier has a fruitier, more volatile perfume. With age, these aromas become "heavier" and more impressive. Expert tasters of Champagne like to talk about the "freshness" of a young wine and the "roundness" of one that is more mature. "Finesse" is also a word that is associated with Champagne. This quality is especially apparent in Champagne that has been made exclusively from the *cuvée* must at pressing time, and when an appreciable proportion of Chardonnay wine is used in the blend.

Champagne's fruitiness is very discreet and depends on the quality of the grapes used. It never impinges on your sense of taste, as does that of a wine such as the German *Gewürztraminer*, it also tends to soften and diminish as the wine ages. The flavour of any Champagne, whether it be dry, fruity or sweet, is always light — professional wine tasters describe it as "long

Producers accept that their customers have very individual preferences when it come to wine, and today the luxury of Champagne can be enjoyed in many forms.

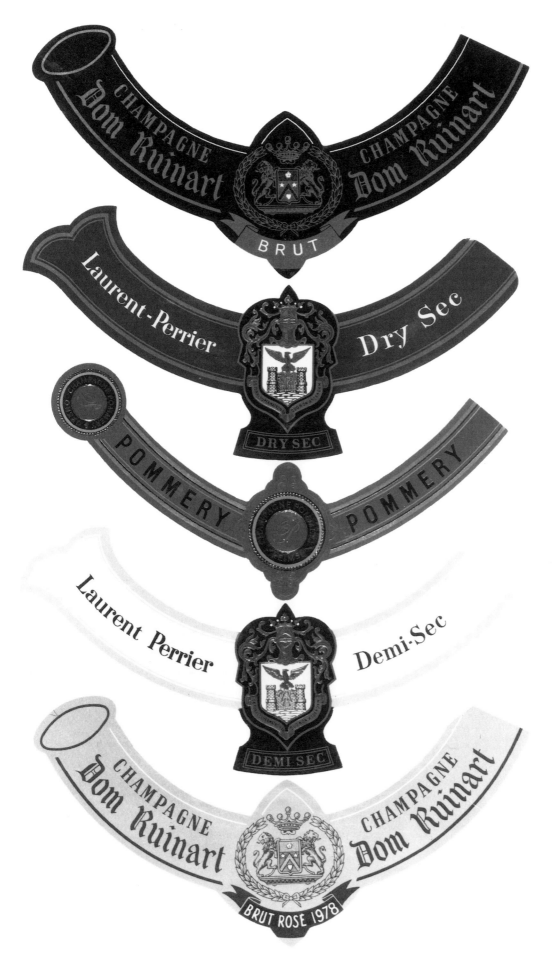

CHAMPAGNE Dom Ruinart · CHAMPAGNE Dom Ruinart
BRUT

Laurent-Perrier · Dry Sec
DRY SEC

POMMERY · POMMERY

Laurent Perrier · Demi-Sec
DEMI SEC

CHAMPAGNE Dom Ruinart · CHAMPAGNE Dom Ruinart
BRUT ROSE 1978

The scrupulous cleanliness, essential to the success of Champagne, is maintained today with as much care as it was in the past. Bottle washing by hand had to be very thorough to ensure that the wine remained pure.

in the mouth". By this, they mean that the flavour lingers on the palate, to be enjoyed for far longer than you might expect.

Great care is taken at every stage of its production to protect Champagne from unwanted or intrusive flavours. Hygiene is of paramount importance. The least defect or impurity, or accidental mishandling, can so severely damage a House's reputation, not to mention its profitability, that the makers are all extraordinarily careful to use fresh corks and sterilized bottles.

Champagne can be badly affected by light, so it is best to keep it away from both sunlight and artificial light as much as possible, until it is ready to be consumed. The bottles are normally made of dark green glass and wrapped in special protective paper, or an opaque coating of plastic film, so insulating the wine from light. Air is another enemy. A bottle of Champagne can lose its taste and become oxidized if it is kept for too long and its cork shrinks, allowing air to enter.

Generally speaking, however, with normal handling and storage, Champagne is a tough product whose qualities are hard to corrupt. As Maurice Healy says in his book

"*Stay Me with Flagons*": "It is the best tempered of all wines: it calls for no coddling and resents no ill treatment. Send a case to the North Pole and then to the Sahara Desert; bring it back to London, finishing the journey in the shakiest of conveyances; give it half an hour in the refrigerator, and it will pour into your glass, not, of course, at its best, but clear and well flavoured and pleasant to drink."

The Champagne tradition

Champagne is a symbol almost everywhere in the world of elegance, happiness and fun. Ever since it was "invented", Champagne has been used for drinking toasts, celebrating business deals, launching ships and business enterpises, and for festivities of all kinds. It has been known to provide artificial rain in Monaco; I poured a bottle of Pommery (oh sacrilege!) down the awning of the Hotel de Paris at the wedding of Grace Kelly and Prince Rainier! At Ascot or Epsom, the horsey set, like their equivalents at Chantilly and Auteuil, Churchill Downs and Belmont Park, celebrate their successes with Champagne.

This festive use of Champagne has spread beyond the Iron Curtain, where Soviet cosmonauts are hailed on their return from space with "Champanski" — the Russian version of the real thing. Even those most ardent and loyal Burgundy fanatics, the *Chevaliers du Tastevin*, will interrupt the ceremonial worship of their excellent red and white wines during the "enthronement" of new members to toast their acolytes with bubbling Champagne.

The fact that imitators abound is, for the Champenois, a rather annoying form of flattery, but it all goes to show just what an astonishingly powerful appeal the wine has for people in all walks of life. Its reputation may be due partly to the way it is publicized as a rare, precious and highly desirable beverage. When I was a schoolboy, one of my colleagues managed to smuggle back a bottle of Champagne from his sister's wedding. He invited his friends to share a

Two stunning Art Deco advertisements for Moët & Chandon's Brut Imperial and Crémant Imperial. The romantically beautiful "goddesses" evoke a luxurious and refined Champagne image.

The classic Champenios method of pouring Champagne – with thumb tucked into the punt and the fingers spread to support the body of the bottle – requires plenty of practice if it is to be executed with style.

sip of this magical elixir. Most of us were thrilled – not so much by the wine, of which there was too little for it to make an impression – but by the *idea* of Champagne. Its glamorous reputation communicated itself to us in a thrill of forbidden pleasure.

Serving Champagne
Opening a bottle of Champagne is always an exciting moment. However, there is a trick to this. Not only is the cork often very tightly embedded in the bottle, but the wine also has a tendency to effervesce copiously and literally explode out of the bottle as the latter is opened. This is because of the power of the pent-up gas Champagne contains, which becomes even more uncontrollable if the bottle has been shaken on its way from the cellar to your table. Some people find this exciting, of course. In the days when military men wore sabres as part of their uniforms, it was considered de rigueur to whisk off the top of a Champagne bottle with a slash of the sword – spectacular perhaps, but rather wasteful in my opinion. If "popping the cork" gives you pleasure, however, then pop away, but, today, the purists remove the cork

with as little noise and waste as possible.

The trick is simple. Just hold the cork tight and twist the bottle carefully. The cork will normally come out with a suppressed "pop", and the wine will stay in the bottle long enough for you to pour the first half glass without its becoming a fountain! I have specified a half glass, because the first drops of Champagne you pour do tend to foam up, despite all precautions. If a glass is filled to the brim, the precious wine will spill over the rim of a full glass, which is a pitiful waste. Pouring a small amount first means that, when you top up the glass, the wine stays inside it – until it goes inside you!

Champagne, too, should be served chilled, rather than icy cold; a really cold Champagne tends to lose some of its precious bouquet. The ideal is to cool the bottle in a Champagne bucket half-filled with water and plenty of ice cubes. For big parties, a tub with the same proportions of water and ice is the best freshener. In an emergency, 10 minutes in the freezer will do the trick, and, most importantly, do the wine no harm. It is very important not to forget your bottle, because it will freeze and explode if left for too long. Twenty minutes in an ordinary refrigerator is a gentler and probably better alternative.

Personally, I find that there is very little to choose between these methods. Sitting a bottle in a cool mountain stream is yet another effective (and very aesthetic!) method of chilling Champagne, but you must tie it to a rock or a tree in case the current deprives you of the refreshing pleasure altogether.

There is a ritual to the actual pouring of the wine as well. When a Champenois pours Champagne, he or she always holds the bottle with a thumb in the punt and fingers on the outside of the bottle to support its weight. The method is impressive, but requires quite a bit of practice if you are to avoid dropping the bottle. A more foolproof method is to clasp the bottle firmly around its girth. Do not wrap the bottle in a towel, though you can wipe it down if it is wet; Champagne is a prestigious wine and people enjoy knowing that they are drinking it. You need never be ashamed of showing your guests the specific pleasure you are offering them.

The best glasses to use these days are the

elegant tulip or the flute, the former being the more practical as its sides curve inwards slightly at the top. This controls the effervescent contents as you lift the glass to your lips, whereas the straighter flute seems to allow the wine to brim over the rim if it is not handled carefully. Both are attractive shapes, however, and show off the slender stream of rising bubbles to their best advantage.

In a really good Champagne, the bubbles are minute, rising seductively in a delicate "necklace" from the bottom of the glass for a surprisingly long time. Indeed, this is one of the instantly recognizable qualities of Champagne. Some sparkling wines not made according to the natural *méthode champenoise* precepts have large, unstable bubbles, which consequently strike the palate as being artificially charged and over-

"Champagne Charlie", a smash hit in 1869, extolling the virtues of Moët & Chandon Champagne, was the first in a succession of tremendously popular British music hall songs, written in honour of the wine.

gaseous. These bubbles also disappear within a minute or two of the wine being poured.

Pink Champagne

I have to admit that pink Champagne is not one of my personal favourites, but its popularity is undeniably growing. Almost all the Champagne Houses produce it in either of two ways: by combining red Champagne wines with white to achieve the desired colour, or by the more difficult method of letting the grape skins stay in the must for a

127

brief period before the wine is taken away
to ferment. The longer the skins and the
juice are combined, the pinker the wine will
be. Pink Champagne produced by blending
must conform to all the standards that
apply to the white variety. A Champagne
House is not permitted to blend a pink
Champagne without notifying the
Champenois tax officials two hours before
the blending begins.

Champagne is the only European wine
that can legally produce pink wine by
blending. This is a long-standing tradition,
and Champagne's pinks have always been
made in this way. At the moment, pink
Champagne represents a fairly minor
percentage of the total amount of
Champagne produced, but most of the best-
known names in Champagne are now
making pink and are looking at the future
through rose-tinted glasses. Pommery is only
one of many pink-producing Houses that
are very satisfied with their version of the
product, and the health of its sales.

When and how to enjoy Champagne
Champagne is a marvellous beverage at any
time of the day or night, but the evening is
probably the time when it sparkles most
effectively. It is the wine for special
occasions. The French mostly drink
Champagne to celebrate weddings and
christenings – nearly 90 per cent of the
French are baptized and married with
Champagne as their ceremonial drink. In
the ordinary way, most people tend to drink
Champagne at the end of a meal. A French
survey found this true of 70 per cent of the
people interviewed. This may well be
because it is often the time when speeches
are made, and Champagne is absolutely
indispensible for drinking toasts.

For end-of-the-meal drinking, choose one
of the less dry varieties of Champagne, so
that its acidity does not present too sharp a
contrast with a sweet dessert. A *sec* or a
demi-sec, despite their names, are perfect.
Brut would be too brutal; tasting almost
bitter compared to a *sec* wine. Older wines,

**A scene of luxurious enjoyment, in which
a party of Victorian gentlemen sample the
delights of Bollinger Champagne. Their
enthusiasm for the wine can be gauged
from the bottles littering the table!**

having mellowed with age, also make a good accompaniment to the meal's end.

According to Alexander Dumas in his *Grand Dictionnaire de Cuisine*: "The wine of Champagne, Sillery *frappé*, is the last wine served, and is to be drunk while eating. If you have no ice, or no Sillery, you should substitute the best sparkling Champagne at your disposal. Cool, uncork and pour. The same glass, as long as it is first emptied, can be used throughout a meal, for all types of Champagne." Sillery, a village on the river Vesle, near Reims, was the best known source of fine Champagne at the time, though much of the wine produced was not only still, but red.

Personally, I prefer to drink Champagne as an aperitif, but breakfast with Champagne, or with a Mimosa – half Champagne, half orange juice – is hard to beat. Winston Churchill, it is said, was a great advocate of a split of Champagne every morning, to start his day off on the best possible footing! A non-vintage *brut* is the wine I would recommend for such early morning indulgence.

There are those who favour Champagne as a "pick-me-up" between meals. In fact, Champagne is generally held to be a solace and a calming influence at times of stress, whenever they occur. It will have a stimulating effect on your conversation and your spirits at almost any time of day. The

Treating your guests with a prestige vintage like "René Lalou" is usually only feasible for small parties. A good non-vintage is usual for a larger gathering.

French dietetic specialist, Dr. E.A. Maury, believes that Champagne is good for us because it has an "euphoric effect on the psyche, without the disadvantages of classic tranquilizers"!

Food and Champagne

The Champagne region is not renowned for its gastronomic prowess, but there are several speciality products and dishes that delight food enthusiasts visiting the area.

The Champenois create a great many dishes based on pork. Bacon, ham and even pig's trotters presented in a variety of traditional ways are definitely *spécialitiés de la région*. Wild boar is still hunted enthusiastically in the forests in and around Champagne, but it is still a rare dish to find on offer except on very special occasions. Sausages of all shapes and sizes, and made from a variety of meats and fish, are, on the other hand, very much daily fare in Champagne, as is *choucroute* (sauerkraut), which is imported from Alsace on its borders.

The cheeses of Champagne are varied and very fine. The most famous of them all is probably Brie, which is made mainly in the west of the region, but the one I find irresistible is the strong, pungent Maroille, produced in the farms to the north-east. Boursault is yet another celebrated local cheese. The *pâtisserie* of the region is particularly good, and it also produces a plentiful amount of fruit, including the famous Rousselet pear, which is said to be so exceedingly juicy that it is almost impossible to handle.

Cooking with Champagne

Champagne imparts its own special flavour to any food, and the regional wine is sometimes used in Champenois recipes. Personally, I cannot help feeling that its flavour is too subtle and its *mousse* too transient, (once heated), for it to be used indiscriminately in cooking. Many restaurants in Champagne make a point of citing Champagne as an ingredient in their dishes, but this is rather more to appeal to their customers' penchant for a touch of luxury than because it revolutionizes the taste of the food. A good white wine will promote much the same flavour in a dish.

However, there are some recipes which include Champagne that I have enjoyed very much. One of these is oysters served in a Champagne sauce, made with cream and egg yolks. The oysters are poached for a few minutes in their own liquid with half a bottle of Champagne. The liquid is then reduced, and the egg and cream whisked into it. This sauce is allowed to thicken. The oysters are served in their cleaned shells with the sauce poured over them. Grilling the oysters for a few moments gives them an attractive golden crust.

Choucroute is sometimes served in a spectacular way by the Champenois. On special occasions, the *choucroute* is cooked with pork, bacon, sausages, and onions and potatoes and presented at the table. At the moment of serving, a quarter bottle of Champagne without its wire muzzle is thrust into its centre. The heat from the cabbage sends the cork shooting out and a fountain of Champagne emerges to drench the food. It is a most entertaining way of serving this rather mundane dish.

These two dishes are exceptionally good, but I still believe that Champagne makes a better accompaniment to food than it does an ingredient in a recipe.

Champagne with food

Champagne is often served as an aperitif at dinner parties or luncheons, because the simple fact of its presence seems to promote relaxation and happiness. Some hosts believe that Champagne also complements any or all foods, and that therefore they need not worry about which wine to serve with each individual dish – from oysters, which are best accompanied by the best of *bruts*, to the dessert, which will require a softer, sweeter variety.

This easy luxury is all very well if you are entertaining only a few guests, but for a larger party, it is more economical, and often better, to provide a range of quality wines that are chosen specifically to accompany certain dishes. Champagne complements the sharp taste of a salad for instance, no better than other wines; nor does it blend successfully with curry, chocolate or very salty food. However, with some foods, especially oysters, Champagne is probably the very best of all possible accompaniments. Some people claim that it is truly ideal when combined with *foie gras*. The English wit of the early 19th century, Sydney Smith, wrote that his "idea of heaven" was "eating *pâté de foie gras* and drinking Champagne to the sound of trumpets". The wine cuts down the richness of such luxury foods to perfectly digestible levels.

Some cheeses, too, go well with Champagne. Roquefort and Stilton, powerful as they are, are good with a *demi-sec*. Brie and some of the hard cheeses, such as Emmenthal, Gruyère and Parmesan, are complemented by a *brut* or an *extra sec*. *Extra sec* is also recommended for fish or meat, while shellfish and hors d'oeuvres are best with *brut*.

For a dinner party, you should count on having a bottle of Champagne for each guest, because these meals tend to stretch out for longer than others. Luncheon usually requires half as much – especially if business is involved. At cocktail time, it is surprising how impressive it is to serve only Champagne – and how surprisingly economical this can be. I attended a reception for about 150 people recently where only Champagne was served, and the hosts were amazed to discover that only four cases of Champagne were consumed during the party – about a third of a bottle per person. Choosing which wine to serve is very much a matter of taste and, of course, budget. For a large party, I would recommend serving a non-vintage wine, but a vintage wine has more prestige if you want to impress a smaller, more discriminating group. This does not mean that vintage wines are necessarily better; indeed many people would choose a non-vintage for preference.

How to treat Champagne

All Champagne is ready to drink when sold, so little is to be expected or gained by storing the wines for longer as far as aging is concerned. It is not even necessary to let them "rest" before drinking, though it is probably wise to do so, just to let them regain their composure. So, Champagne is convenient to buy, by the case or the bottle, depending on the available cellar space. Under the right conditions, the wine will retain its perfection for many a year.

I have drunk a Champagne that had been kept in its original cellars for 72 years. It was slightly maderized – brownish in colour, with a delicious aroma and a slightly sweetish taste. Upon opening, its sparkle was as sprightly as you could wish, although it lasted for only a few moments. However, this was in a special circumstance. To try to keep such an old wine in a drinkable state, it really has to live in ideal conditions, without much movement, since it was first filled. In this instance, I have to admit that the makers of the Champagne I tasted had to open four or five ancient bottles before finding one in a drinkable condition.

Old is not necessarily best in Champagne terms. Normally, Champagne begins to age beyond the ideal in about five to seven years after its purchase, in other words, about 15 years from the time it was first fermented. So there is nothing to be gained by laying down Champagne in the same way you might a Bordeaux or a Burgundy wine, to pass on to your children and grandchildren.

Like any other wine, Champagne should be stored on its side so that the cork is always moist and prevents any air from seeping into the wine. It should also be kept away from light and never kept anywhere where the temperature might reach more than 10 or 12°C (50 or 54°F). Your care will be rewarded when you taste the wine.

Choosing the wine

There is no such thing as a "best" Champagne brand – it all comes down to personal preference. If you have no favourite brand of your own, ask the advice of someone who knows the wine well. Having tasted several different types, you will probably be able to make up your own mind about the flavour, the age and the degree of sweetness you prefer. Taittinger has a reputation for very dry wines, Bollinger and Krug for fruity ones, and Veuve Clicquot for a tendency to richness, but the latter three can all have a dry quality. The choice is wide and fascinating.

At least, with Champagne, the knotty business of vintages in less important than it is for many other wines; this is because of the blending that the "ordinary" Champagne undergoes. A vintage Champagne may have its own particular flavour, selected because the maker feels that his wine crop that year has been particularly fine, but a blended wine can usually be depended upon to give you the same flavour bottle after bottle, and year after year.

Cocktails

Personally, I prefer my Champagne straight, but there are some delicious cocktails that can be made from it. There is the "Bellini", made with 56ml (2fl oz) of peach juice (fresh if possible), 13ml (4fl oz) of ice-cold Champagne, and a dash of Grenadine, mixed in a large wine glass. "Black Velvet" is also very good and very simple: half proportions of Guinness stout and Champagne. A "Buck's Fizz" is 95ml (3–4fl oz) of non-vintage Champagne with one 28ml (1fl oz) of fresh orange juice and a dash of grenadine. My favourite is a cocktail made with 28ml (1fl oz) of Cognac, 113ml (4fl oz) of iced Champagne and a twist of orange peel. Pour the brandy into a large wine glass, add the Champagne, and twist the orange peel across the rim of the glass as a tangy decoration. The recipe is simple and the taste delicious.

An intimate group of friends enjoy a _rosé_ Champagne in this lovely 1893 watercolour sketch. Champagne is still indispensible for many private as well as public celebrations.

Champagne Today

Champagne's business affairs have rejoiced in almost "habitual prosperity", as Colonel François Bonal, one of Champagne's most respected experts, puts it in his excellent 500-page "encyclopedia" of Champagne. There are a total of some 110 *négociants-manipulants*, who all make their own wine, often from their own vineyards, which they may or may not sell under their own brand name. Many of these producers, although small, are well established. New Champagne producers are rare. Good vineyard property is so scarce that only 4–5ha (10 acres) of it are offered for sale in any one year, and the asking price is around two million francs per hectare. If this was not enough to discourage newcomers, there is not any real "market" for a new wine farmer to tap.

The firm foundations
Champagne has several *syndicats* of the various elements in the organization of its wine industry. Their purpose is to establish rules about the optimum way of growing vines; to protect the good name of Champagne from counterfeits or imitations; and to help settle disagreements within the industry. One of the most important of these syndicates is that of the *Grandes Marques*. To become a member, a firm must be making Champagne only under its own name or brands. This means that "Buyer's Own Brand" producers, who will make you a Champagne to your own specifications if you can afford it, cannot be part of this élite group, unless they are very large organizations able to buy one of the *Grande Marque* wines.

The annual shipments of a *Grande Marque* firm must amount to no less than 0.5 per cent of the total for all the Champagne shipped yearly. Its product must be a blend, or *cuvée*, of "constant quality", and the House must have an established reputation. Changes in management, or sales fall off, may result in loss of membership. The dozen or so present members of the *Syndicat de Grandes Marques* control more than three-quarters of all Champagne business, and over 85 per cent of its ever-expanding export trade.

These Houses, or groupings of Houses are:
Moët & Chandon, Mercier and *Ruinart* (which are grouped under the holding company, Moët-Hennessy).
G.H. Mumm, Heidsieck Monopole and *Perrier-Jouët* (which all belong to Seagrams of Canada).
Piper-Heidsieck.
Lanson and *Pommery* (a part of the French BSN food group).
Veuve Clicquot-Ponsardin, Canard-Duchêne and *Henriot*.
Laurent Perrier and *Lemoine*.
Taittinger and *Irroy*.
Charles Heidsieck and *Krug* (part of the Remy Martin group).
Louis Roederer.

Of these, six alone do about half the total Champagne business – Moët, Mumm, Piper-Heidsieck, Pommery, Taittinger and Veuve Clicquot.

Fifteen per cent of Champagne's business is done by the next layer of Houses. There are 20 of these, but they ship only about six per cent of the total Champagne production. The remainder of the output is divided between the rest of the *négociants-manipulants*, the *récoltants-manipulants*, (grower-producers), the co-operatives, the Houses, *négociants-non-manipulant*, that make wines for other sales organizations – "Buyer's Own Brand", or BOBs, and independent small growers, who either sell grapes to others, or make and sell their own wines.

"Buyer's Own Brand" Champagne
There has been a good deal of confusion and argument over "Buyer's Own Brand" wines. The practice of having wines "made to order", so to speak, has been going on, and been accepted, by the Champagne industry for many years. If you can afford it, and need something special for a particular market, or for your own use, you can have it – at a price. Being a blend, Champagne *can* be made to order. Whether the wine used in a *cuvée* is made "in house", or by someone else, makes no more difference to the final result than does the blending of various wines, as long as the quality of the finished wine is up to standard.

The biggest BOB producers tend to sell their highest quality wines under a label of their own. Most producers sell their vintages year after year to the same marketing organization. The reason for this is a matter of simple economics – they get better prices than they would if they tried to sell their output themselves. When a House buys from a BOB producer, the House has its own wine experts work with the BOB establishment on the *assemblage* of the grapes used for the *cuvée*.

BOB producers' success, however, can see-saw up and down depending on the state of the industry's stocks. When a harvest is poor, controlled quality grapes from peripheral growers are needed and used by all producers, including the big Houses and the BOB firms. Everyone is affected by a poor harvest and the demand for grape stocks is universal.

BOB wine is often young because many of the producers are small growers, and do not have the storage capacity to hold the wine after it has reached the minimum age of the one year. There is no lasting guarantee of quality either. Many hotels, restaurants, marketing organizations and chain stores outside France market their own private brands of Champagne. Since the brand name belongs to them, they are at liberty to change their suppliers from year to year. The result can be that a private brand name's quality could vary somewhat dramatically from year to year but here again, the French laws provide the drinker with a fair degree of protection.

Strict regulations determine the correct labelling of Champagne bottles so that customers can be certain that the wines they buy are the genuine article. The origin of every bottle has to be declared on its label.

How regulations prevent controversy
There can be no trickery or scandal concerning the use of BOBs, according to Colonel Bonal, because: "Champagne is too strictly regulated". For example, every Champagne label, including those of BOB makers, must, according to French law, include a combination of letters and numbers that allow the consumer, if he wishes, to check the exact provenance of every bottle. The designation gives a couple of initials, followed by a serial number. The initials indicate what type of manufacturer produced the wine. They include:

NM – for *Négociant-Manipulant* – marketing producer
MA – *Marque Auxiliaire* – a subsidiary label
RM – *Récoltant-Manipulant* – a grower who makes and sells his own wine
CM – *Co-opérative-Manipulant* – a co-op that makes its own brands.

The figures that follow the initials give further information about which maker produced the bottle. For instance, a bottle of Deutz, "Cuvée William Deutz," vintage 1979 bears the numbers NM2.736.392, and a Louis Roederer, *brut* non-vintage, NM.364.242. If you cite these figures to the

CIVC, it can check who produced the wine, where it came from and what the wine is.

What all this means is that a maker cannot avoid responsibility for what is in a bottle marked with an official label. An overseas marketeer might replace the French label with one of his own, although it is unlikely that he would do so. The sheer nuisance value of such a procedure would tend to inhibit such an activity – and, besides, it would be illegal.

The volume of BOB business, according to some Champenois, has reached its peak. If too much is made, quality is undermined and the glut prejudices established sales. The best BOB wines are all spoken for, which tends to inhibit anyone trying to break into the BOB market and the sales balance is kept constant. Buying from independent operators may be less costly than buying from a well-known *Marque* producer, (since they have few overheads, their prices are almost 40 per cent lower), but this practice is rewarding only if you are a smart taster, and can afford the time to select your wine with care. The main problem for a buyer who may be tempted to work with an independent is that, since the majority are small operators, the independent producers sometimes have trouble maintaining the quality and flavour of their wines. They sell mainly *mono-cru*, or one-vineyard, Champagnes, which can vary in quality from one year to the next because of the producers' limited capacity. The possibilities for blending are inhibited by the variations in their local micro-climates and their limited supply of grapes, so it is impossible to ensure the consistency of any wine.

The independent brands
There are well over 5000 different brand names to choose from. About half the amount of wine produced for these brands is made by people who treat their vineyards as a sideline and a supplementary source of income. In addition, over the years there have developed dozens of amalgamations of firms; new, smaller firms; and hundreds of inter-marriages between members of different companies. It becomes almost impossible for someone outside the region to keep track of the quality of many of the lesser known labels.

The largest of the independent *négociants-non-manipulants*, is one of which most people have never heard – *Marne et Champagne* of Epernay. This house makes 10 million bottles of Champagne a year, sold under hundreds of private labels, one of which, "A. Rothschild", alone accounts for two million bottles. The wines are sold to a number of marketing organizations, chain stores, department stores or brand owners from around the world.

Additional established BOB producers include the *Société Anonyme de Magenta-Epernay* (SAME), which also owns the brand "De Casenove". A. Charbaut & Fils supplies wines to various restaurants in France under their own labels, and to Sainsbury's supermarket chain in the UK. Duval-Leroy sells good BOB wines that make up three-quarters of its total production. Two other well known BOB brands are Bruno Paillard and Henriot.

The co-operatives
Many of the *co-opératives* sell on a BOB basis. If you are thinking of offering your own private label Champagne at your next party, why not taste what these producers have to offer. The *Centre Vinicole de la Champagne* is a co-op to which other co-ops belong! One of the brands it handles is Nicholas Feuillate. The *Co-opérative de l'Union Champagne* (in addition to its own brand "Saint Gall") supplies Marks & Spencers chain stores in the UK and other BOB customers. Some co-ops have unfortunately long names – *Union Auboise des Producteurs de Vins de Champagne; Co-opérative Vinicole de Mancy, Société de Producteurs Mailly-Champagne; Société Co-opérative de Producteurs des Grandes Territoires de Champagne; Co-opérative de Champagnisation des Côteaux du Val de la Marne* – and so on.

There are some 146 co-ops scattered around the region at places like Mailly, Avize, Reims and Vertus. Some co-ops only press grapes and sell the must; others both press and turn the must into wine. Some co-ops sell a finished, dosed wine, ready to be labelled by BOB owners.

The controversial practice of selling wines *sur lattes* – that is, wine that has been bottled, but is still un-disgorged, and is ready to have *dosage* added, then be labelled and presented for sale – is considered a false

problem by responsible producers. Such wines cannot easily be tasted or checked for quality, since they are already in bottles. Theoretically, they could be given a *dosage* to change their taste, but no reputable brand will run the risk of buying wine in that state without knowing what it contained. They buy, when necessary, only from bulk *cuvées* before bottling, which they themselves can supervise, thus guaranteeing that the resulting wine is as good as their own.

Wines *sur lattes* can, of course, be sold to shippers or marketing organizations which resell them under their own labels. It is up to the shippers to make sure that the quality of such wines accords with their claims and that the blend remains consistent from year to year.

Champagne has enjoyed its reputation as a quality wine for many years. This stylish Victorian gentleman obviously appreciates that it is the perfect wine to make the right impression on his lady companion.

By this token, wines that are marketed simply with the name of a grower on the label are likely to be less reliable than those of a known brand. Since one man and his wife can handle about 2½ha (6 acres) of vineyard, and live "quite well" on their produce, according to Monsieur Geoffroy of the *Co-opérative de l'Union Champagne*, there are hundreds of such small-holdings. Each vineyarder makes his wine differently so you may enjoy experimenting to find a

good product. However, if you return the next year for "the same again", you may discover to your disappointment that it is not the same thing at all.

Tasting

Because of the sheer scale of Champagne production, to find out which brand suits your palate best as a regular beverage, a certain amount of practice in judging the quality of wine is required. The only way to achieve this is through tasting. The easiest way to taste a variety of Champagnes is to take a trip through the Champagne country. Almost any House, or local roadside producer, will be glad to give you a sip of its product.

Tasting is an acquired skill. The procedures for tasting Champagne are no different from those for any other wine – the eye, the nose and the palate are all brought into play. The huge majority of Champagne is white, with a few pinks thrown in nowadays. There is no red Champagne to confuse the issue. Thus the eye has to detect subtle differences between very similar looking wines, and the palate has to distinguish between small variations in excellence.

Comparisons between the best brands must take into account one's own preferences. Except in extraordinary cases, such as when a bottle is "corked", can these Champagnes be considered as anything but near perfection – the very best that its maker can achieve. Any Champagne tasting is a contest of superstars.

Sensual checkpoints

The first thing to do in tasting, ironically enough is to use your eyes. Clearness is essential and I have never seen an "unlimpid" Champagne. Except in almost inconceivable circumstances, all sediment will have been discovered and eliminated long before you taste the wine. Champagne's colour should be of pale straw if the wine is young, the colour becoming more and more golden as the wine ages

Ideally, tasting should take place in a quiet, scrupulously clean, well lit environment. But visitors to the Champagne region enjoy sampling its wines at the various *dégustation* centres.

until it is deep golden. Unless you have been keeping Champagne too long in your own cellars (say for over 10 years) and in the wrong conditions, it should never become the colour of Madeira. A further visual checkpoint is the *mousse*. Bubbles should be tiny, and stream up continuously from the bottom of the glass.

The next activity in tasting is to use your nose. A sniff will tell you that the wine is fresh and grapey, and therefore young, or that it has a fuller flavour and is therefore a mature wine.

Finally you actually "taste". Take a sip and hold it in your mouth while you draw in a breath to aerate the wine, and emphasize the flavour it holds. Use your palate and tongue to tell you if the wine is very dry, crisp and light, or slightly sweet, tasting, as well as smelling, of its fruit, and stimulatingly full of flavour.

TASTING TERMS

Wine tasters need a special vocabulary to describe a wine's taste and aroma. To understand the terms used it is essential to have a good imagination and to have tasted a good many Champagnes. Here are a few indicators:

Full – *which includes assertive, meaty, mature, rich, weighty, big, nutty.*
Crisp – *includes light, dry, young, fragrant.*
Rich – *sweet, soft, flowery.*
Medium – *when you can't make up your mind, understated.*
Elegant – *reliable, has breeding.*
Complex – *stimulating, distinctive.*

Tasting terms are a sort of shorthand through which experts, and sometimes knowledgeable and experienced amateurs, try to communicate their impressions about Champagne. I must admit that I am among those who find Champagne difficult to "taste". The first sip causes the bubbles to foam up alarmingly in my mouth and thereby prevent any clear impression of the wine's flavour. At the next sip – probably as a result of the bubbles again – I tend to hiccup, which is not only undignified, but makes it difficult to suck in the wine with tiny breaths of air so as to allow the full flavours to float over the palate. However, this does not in the least prevent me from enjoying Champagne to the full!

The best Champagne will "finish well" – that is, the final sip should leave a fresh, agreeable taste on your palate. "When they have finished actually tasting, professionals will breathe out hard", says one of the best of tasters, Pamela Vandyke Price. "This enables them to discover the after-taste and smell which should remind them of, and confirm, their first impressions."

Learn to trust your judgment
Your own tastes will develop with experience. What you liked last year may not appeal to you in the same way a year later. Whatever happens, enjoyment of Champagne is a totally personal matter. The way the wine tastes to you is all that is important. If you like it, drink it, and don't worry about what anyone else says.

There is not much point, either, in comparing one Champagne to another, for again the styles may not be comparable. You may like a mature, full-bodied, serious wine. I may prefer a light, fragrant one. We are both right.

Comparative tasting
The CIVC and the Champagne producers as a body, are not enchanted by the idea of comparative tastings. They claim that serious tasting should take place only in optimum conditions – without any extraneous odours or noise; clean glasses; and good light. Only then can an objective opinion about a wine be given. Most tastings are done subjectively – tasters' appreciations often differ, as do the wine's styles. "Establishing a hierarchy of Champagnes on the basis of comparative tasting," say the Champenois, "is about as sensible as asking music lovers to rank composers, or art lovers to state that Monet is superior or inferior to Picasso. One's choice of Champagne should be a matter of personal taste alone".

To help in the process of personal taste selection it might be useful to learn something about what a wine taster would want to know about the Champagne he or she was trying. Even professional tasters often come up with completely different opinions about the same wines. These differences should be disregarded because impressions of a particular *cuvée* change if it is served at different temperatures or from different bottles. A wine taster can rationalize personal feeling about a Champagne in this way, whatever the opinion of his or her colleagues.

To illustrate this point, the Swiss tell a story of two compatriots meeting after a day's work. One of them had just been fired, the other had had a salary increase. So they decided to commiserate and celebrate together with a bottle of Champagne. The first man complained about his glass. His companion liked his. So they agreed to order a second bottle just to test their first reactions. By the end of this bottle, they still disagreed so they opened a third. Such inability to decide is the reason why the Swiss sales of Champagne, they say, are so successful!

Vintages
Vintage Champagne is made only from the grapes and the wine gathered and produced from a single harvest, but is not necessarily an indication of the best Champagne. A vintage Champagne cannot be blended with wines from other years, as is the case with most Champagne. That is why a Champagne House is never judged by its vintage product. (Champagne differs in this respect from wines like those of Bordeaux or Burgundy, which carry a vintage date, whether or not the particular harvest was good.)

In Champagne the choice of naming a vintage or not is up to the individual producer – it does not apply, necessarily, to the whole area. A Bordeaux or Burgundy "vintage" may command double the usual price for its wine. A Champagne vintage is also more expensive than non-vintage, but there is not such a startling difference between their prices.

London's famed Victorian Champagne expert Henry Vizitelli, wrote in 1879 that his investigations indicated a great vintage could be expected only twice in a decade. Between 1800 and 1900, 23 good vintages, have been recorded so Vizitelli's guess seems to have been right in his lifetime. Champagne makers may decide,

individually, to declare a vintage. Sometimes, if the growing conditions have been exceptional, they might even agree unanimously on a "vintage year".

The golden years
The most famous vintage of the 19th century, or of any since, was in 1815 – the year of Halley's Comet – a year that was superb, both for quantity and quality. Naturally, this Champagne was dubbed "The Wine of the Comet". Echoes of this striking year linger on in the form of the

These Moët & Chandon vintage Champagnes were both outstanding. The year 1914 marked the end of the era, but its vintage Champagne is still considered to have been one of the best this century.

comet motif that is printed on many bottle labels, and stamped on the ends of Champagne corks.

1846 and 1874 were two other great years. None remains to taste, but contemporary experts were ecstatic about the Champagnes produced. Later, during the "Belle Epoque" period in Paris at the end of the 19th century, vintages were announced in 1889, 1892, 1893, 1898 and 1899. Maxim's Restaurant opened during this period and became the place where the best of Champagnes were drunk, often in the company of the most beautiful of ladies – Caroline Otero, Cléo de Mérode, Emelienne d'Alençon, Lian de Pougy, and other notorious beauties of the *haute* and *demi-mondes*. It was rumoured that they lived on Champagne. They certainly preferred it to water and persuaded a great many other people to share their taste.

After the turn of the century, the years 1900, 1905, 1907, 1908, 1911, 1913, 1914 and 1915, saw the production of first class wines. They were still very sweet wines compared to those produced today and were usually drunk with desserts. The 1914 vintage was especially fine and was well enough made to be still drinkable in the 1970s. This could have something to do with the fact that the grapes were picked early for fear that the Germans might attack. The acidity of these grapes helped to preserve the wine.

In the Second World War, the vineyards escaped comparatively unscathed, because the German attack broke through along the Aisne and Seine rivers, bypassing Champagne for the most part. Also, the Germans were driven out so quickly at the end of the war, that there was no time for widespread malicious destruction. 1943 was an exceptional vintage. Since then, the best of the declared vintage years have been 1947, 1955, 1964, 1971, and 1982.

The face of Champagne today

When I first got to know Champagne, during the 1950s, the area devoted to vines was less than half what it is today. There are a great many more grapes being grown, and much more wine being made now. There were about 13,000 *vignerons* working only 11,700ha (28,910 acres) of vines before the Second World War. Today there around 15,000 who, with the aid of mechanization, work some 23,000ha (56,830 acres) of vineyard. Because of improvement in the care taken with the making of Champagne, not only has quantity increased, but quality has as well. If the criterion for quality is "declared"

vintages, the improvement is clear – a vintage was declared, (though not always over the whole area), every year from 1969 through to 1982.

VINTAGES

Vintage Champagnes are made only from the wines of a single year when the Houses concerned decide that those wines have particular qualities which make them exceptional. Not all Houses make vintage wines in any particular vintage year.

CHAMPAGNE VINTAGES SINCE 1900

1900	1953
1904	1955
1906	1959
1911	1961
1914	1962
1915	1964
1917	1966
1919	1969*
1921	1970
1923	1971*
1928	1973
1929	1974†
1934	1975
1937	1976
1941	1977†
1943	1978
1945	1979
1947	1980
1949	1981
1952	1982

* *Exceptional*
† *only Roederer*

The greater extent of the vineyards and the improvements in the manufacturers' techniques are not the only changes that have occured in Champagne. The Houses are continually experimenting with new blends to accommodate the increasingly wide range of tastes. "The trend of taste these days," says Monsieur Cense of Mumm, "seems to be towards lighter, more elegant wines than before. In the past, the fruity, more pronounced flavour was what people liked. Tastes change. A 1979

Champagne seems sweeter than its younger brothers because its taste is 'rounder'. It is healthy to maintain a range of wines to ring the flavour changes. A Champagne made with 50 per cent black Pinot grapes has a rich taste. A 100 percent Pinot Noir wine is even richer, with a strong, and tasty flavour, and is considered 'undrinkable' in the USA, while in the UK it is one of the favourite brands".

Although Champagne's style has changed considerably since the Second World War, non-vintage *brut* Champagne is still the criterion by which most experts judge the quality of a Champagne House, being the *vin ordinaire* of the Champagne world. More of this *brut* is made than any other type of Champagne. A *brut* Champagne is considered to have the most acceptable flavour nowadays. Its drier versions, the *sauvages*, the *brut zéros* or the *brut non-dosages* are still only gradually gaining in popularity. The different varieties of *brut* make up an amazing nine-tenths of the total sales of Champagne wines.

The *doux* style of Champagne has disappeared almost entirely. *Rosé* has suddenly become extremely popular and is very much in fashion, though the French seem to think it only a passing one. According to some producers, the French just won't drink it. Raymond Oliver, the founder and owner of the renowned Parisian restaurant, the "Grand Véfour", considers pink Champagne to be "merely a fancy wine". Nevertheless, people find it a fine excuse for self-indulgence and frivolity, and the Champenois are never averse to catering to the desires of their customers. Almost all of Champagne's main producers are making it and finding that it sells particularly well in export markets. So, yet again, if you enjoy it, drink it, regardless of anyone else's opinion.

Crémant is another fairly popular type of Champagne. It is a wine that has only about half the carbon-dioxide of standard Champagne, and therefore it is less effervescent. However, its days are numbered. An agreement has been made whereby the producers of French sparkling wine will have the exclusive right to call their wines *crémant*. In return for this privilege, they have agreed not to claim that their wines are made by the *méthode champenoise*. True Champagne therefore gains a further measure of prestige.

Several Houses have a distinctive "style" of their own that runs through their entire line. Krug, for example, produces fine old-fashioned wines with a rich, mellow taste and a deep, complex flavour while Bollinger's wines are classic, mature and often pleasantly fruity. Along with Deutz, Mumm, Veuve Clicquot, Salon, Ruinart, Roederer and Perrier-Jouët, (to name but a few), Krug and Bollinger are Houses that tend to stick to the full, rounded, weighty, old-time style of Champagne. Those who favour the lighter side of the spectrum include Piper-Heidsieck, Laurent Perrier, Pol Roger, Taittinger, Lanson, Giesler, Charles Heidsieck and Joseph Perrier. Taittinger produces a dry, elegant rather austere type of wine. Both general types are marvellous in their way. It is up to the individual to decide for himself which style he or she prefers.

Sheer decadence
Special Champagne *cuvées* are now made by many Houses. They have no specific regulations as to their production. Their prestige rests on their producers' claims that they are made from specific vineyards, or using only certain combinations of especially fine basic wines. In fact they are simply sales gimmicks, and very successful ones at that. Special *cuvées* are usually packaged in unusually shaped, or decorated bottles. The "granddaddy" of them all was probably Roederer's "Cristal" Champagne with its clear crystal punt-less bottle.

Strangely, enough none of the other Houses began to imitate the idea until Robert de Vogüé came up with the idea of the Dom Pérignon bottle, a copy of an old one that had been found in Moët's cellars. The principle was swiftly followed by other Houses. Perrier-Jouët brought out its pretty, flower-decorated "Belle Epoque" special. Taittinger has one robed in gold, others have had modern artists design their "special" bottles for them. There are at least 30 brands that present a special *cuvée* bottle today. But the majority of Champagne is still contained in the original, punted bottle, decorated with different colourful labels – Mumm's red sash, De Castellane's red cross of St. Antoine, Deutz's red, white and green, and Veuve Clicquot's orange-peel yellow.

Epilogue

The more you learn about the Champagne industry, the more it gives the impression of being one big, more or less happy family. Over the centuries, there have been so many intermarriages between members of the different Champagne Houses that an amazing number of the people in the industry seem to be related, or to have at least one ancestor in common. Certainly, the Champagne makers all seem to know each other, or about each other, and see each other often. It is difficult to go into one of the many excellent restaurants in Reims or Epernay, without running into the principal officers of several Champagne Houses, or independent producers and growers – usually entertaining privileged clients or international journalists. They may be rivals in business, but they all seem to get along very well socially.

The industry's new face
Comte de Vogüé, who was head of Moët & Chandon after the last World War, sparked off the new trend towards the establishment of huge corporate combinations and diversifications. Moët first combined with Mercier, then with Ruinart, and later with Hennessy, and Dior perfumes. Soon, other Champagne Houses followed suit: Krug combined with Remy Martin and Charles Heidsieck; and Perrier-Jouët with Heidsieck Monopole and Seagrams. Several Champagne Houses today also own and operate vineyards in the USA and Australia, and some are involved with wine production in Bordeaux, Burgundy and the Loire.

New blood has been brought into the region recently from America, Great Britain, the Netherlands and Germany. These new managers and owners have brought with them many new marketing ideas, and have changed some aspects of the Champagne industry.

Changing tastes
Although the traditionally cordial atmosphere remains unaltered, the Champagne industry is gradually changing under the impact of corporate growth. In years gone by when the fashionable flavour for Champagne was sweet, no-one would have dreamt that a day would come when sybaritic jet-setters would demand totally dry Champagne. But that day has now come. Hedonists can buy and imbibe a sugarless *brut zéro* "bubbly" without worrying that the effect might eventually force them to slip their belts down a notch or two! They may need to cut out a few other indulgences, but they no longer have to worry about the calories in Champagne.

These "austere" wines cater both to those consumers whose tastes favour the driest of wines, and those unfortunate people who suffer from an inability to digest sugar. The producers, in their desire to keep up with new tastes, have developed this area of the market. On the whole the vogue for dry Champagne is regarded as a positive step towards a greater appreciation of the wine's potential for lightness and delicacy, which until recently was masked by the old-fashioned craze for sweetness. The connoisseurs of Champagne today say that sugar blurs the palate and the bone dry Laurent Perrier "Ultra Brut", and Piper Heidsieck's "Brut Sauvage", are rated as two of the best Champagnes.

There are now speciality dry wines too. This trend was set in motion with the launching of Moët & Chandon's "Dom Pérignon", the first speciality *cuvée* in a uniquely-designed bottle since Roederer's "Cristal" of the early 19th century. Nearly all the other producers have followed the lead. The list of extra-special *cuvées* is long:

The end of a hard day's work at harvest time in the vineyards near Bouzy. The pickers work flat out to ensure that the grapes are brought in quickly to the presses, before they ripen beyond the optimum stage.

Taittinger's "Comtes de Champagne"; Ruinart's "Dom Ruinart"; Clicquot's "Carte d'Or"; Laurent Perrier's "Le Grand Siècle": Krug's "Grande Cuvée"; Bollinger's "Tradition"; Piper-Heidsieck's "Vintage Rare"; A. Rothschild's "Brut Réserve"; Perrier-Jouet's "Belle Epoque"; Mumm's "René Lalou"; and Deutz's "Cuvée William Deutz" to name some of the best. This trend will undoubtedly continue well into the future because it has given a terrific boost to Champagne sales.

Devotion to Champagne

The French, and not least the Champenois, are among the world's most experienced drinkers of wine, and are perhaps its greatest fans. As a nation, they have a healthy respect for wine and for connoisseurship. The Champenois feel that the palm of honour in respect of appreciation of their wine must go to the British. This opinion is not completely unjustified, since Britain has been the major export market for Champagne for many years, and the luxurious wine has become the hallmark of good living and exquisite taste. Describing someone as having "Champagne tastes" is a great Champenois compliment, implying that such a person appreciates the best in everything.

On the other hand, the Champenois regard Americans as being impulsive, rather inconsistent Champagne drinkers. They give the Americans credit for their preference for *brut* over the sweeter wines, and they are very impressed by the fact they buy so much of the more costly special *cuvées*. But the national consumption of Champagne in 1986 was a mere 15,854,468 bottles, and the Champenois feel that such an amount was unworthy of a population of some 250 million! The population of Luxembourg is only 400,000, and the little country imports 400,000 bottles of Champagne a year – by comparison, the Americans appear almost teetotal.

Enjoying the wine

The rate of consumption that the Champenois admire is that demonstrated by a certain Welby Jourdan, once a regular at Maxim's in Paris, who, with two companions, managed to drink 12 magnums of Champagne in the space of five hours. This exuberance obviously did no harm to

Champagne's reputation, nor to Mr Jourdan's health, since he lived to the ripe old age of 94 – positive proof if any were needed that Champagne is good for you! It is certainly true that its euphoric effect need have no unpleasant side-effects, either while drinking it or the morning after, Champagne has just enough alcohol and sparkle to lift your spirits to a joyful level.

For this reason as much as any other, Champagne has always been a celebrity among wines, immortalized by poets and writers alike. A key chorus in Johann Strauss's *Die Fledermaus* is devoted to its praise. "The whole world recognizes King Champagne the First, the king of wine," cry the principals, and the chorus responds: "A toast to the king of wine." Whereupon another character sings: "Drink down and sing the praises of Champagne's many graces!"

Lord Byron was more direct. In a letter to Lady Melbourne in 1812, he writes quite unequivocally: "A woman should never be seen eating or drinking unless it be lobster salad and Champagne." More recently, Alfred Duff Cooper, in his autobiography, "Old Men Forget", writes of reading "Alice in Wonderland" at his club, with "an imperial pint of Champagne, that admirable measure, which like so many good things, has disappeared from the world . . . Whether it was the humour of Lewis Caroll or the sparkle of the widow Clicquot that restored my spirits would be hard to say. I think it was the mating of the two."

A persisting appeal

Champagne is many things to many people. Young people tend to see it as something rare for special occasions, a wine of privilege. Older people may see it more as an indication of friendship, pleasure and elegance. Whatever the reason, Champagne will continue to be enjoyed all over the world at times of special rejoicing – or simply when people want to indulge themselves in little sparkling luxury.

A dry Champagne, such as Laurent Perrier's "Sans Sucre", would, in 1897, have tasted far sweeter than an equivalent *brut* nowadays, catering as it did to established popular taste.

Footman: A glass of Champagne Sir!
Nobleman: No thanks, I dare not drink it,
Host: Don't be afraid! try Laurent-Perrier "Sans-Sucre"
and you will change your mind.

SPECIAL CHAMPAGNE CUVÉES

Ayala & Cie.	Vintage Dom Ruinart Blanc de Blancs Brut
Billecart-Salmon	Vintage Brut Cuvée N.F. Billecart Millésime
Bollinger	Vintage RD
Canard-Duchene	Charles VII Brut
A. Charbaut & Fils	Vintage Certificate Blanc de Blancs Brut
De Castellane	Vintage Commodore
André Drappier	Vintage Grande Sendrée Brut
Deutz & Geldermann	Vintage Cuvée William Deutz
Duval-Leroy	Cuvée du Roys Brut
Gosset	Grande Millésime
George Goulet	Vintage Cuvée du Centenaire
Henriot	Cuvée "Baccarat"
Heidsieck & Cie. Monopole	Vintage Cuvée Diamant Bleu
Charles Heidsieck	Vintage Cuvée "Champagne Charlie" Brut
Piper-Heidsieck	Vintage Rare Vintage Florens-Louis Brut
Krug & Cie.	Grande Cuvée Brut
Lanson Père & Fils	Vintage Noble Cuvée de Lanson Brut
Laurent Perrier & Cie.	Cuvée Grand Siècle
Moët & Chandon	Vintage Dom Pérignon Brut
G. H Mumm & Cie.	Vintage René Lalou Brut
Joseph Perrier	Cuvée Cent Cinquantenaire Brut
Philipponnat	Vintage Clos des Goisses
Pol Roger & Cie.	Vintage Réserve Speciale PR Brut Vintage Cuvée Sir Winston Churchill Brut
Pommery & Greno	Louise Pommery
Louis Roederer	Vintage Cristal Brut
Ruinart Père & Fils	Vintage Dom Ruinart Blanc de Blancs Brut
Taittinger	Vintage Comtes de Champagne Blanc de Blancs Brut
Veuve Clicquot-Ponsardin	Vintage Grande Dame Brut

TRENDS IN FLAVOUR OF THE DIFFERENT CHAMPAGNE BRANDS

Ayala & Cie.
light, clean; some rich and fruity

Besserat de Bellefont
reliable; a French favourite; light, fresh

Bollinger
elegant finesse; traditional; classic; ages well

Deutz & Geldermann
delicate; big flavour in non-vintages; excellent Blanc de Blancs vintage

Alfred Gratien
perfumed, full, mature

Charles Heidsieck
light, fragrant, aromatic; vintages age well

Heidsieck & Cie. Monopole
agreeable well-made non-vintages; fine de luxe cuvée

Krug & Cie.
heady, weighty, distinctive, fruity; full, yet austere; has breeding

Lanson Père & Fils
soft, flowery, fragrant; good aperitif

Laurent Perrier & Cie.
light, refreshing, elegant; ages well

Mercier
fruity, dependable, understated; a French favourite

Moët & Chandon
dependable non-vintage, good vintages; excellent Dom Perignon

G.H. Mumm & Cie.
inclined towards fullness

Joseph Perrier
flowery, delicate; good aperitif

Perrier-Jouët
full, stimulating

Philipponnat
light, dry, soft, perfumed

Piper-Heidsieck
light, aperitif; good finish

Pol Roger & Cie.
light non-vintage; classic vintage

Pommery & Greno
long, dry, full-flavoured

Louis Roederer
depth; great length; rosé; rich, full, round

Ruinart Pere & Fils
elegant, fresh, refined

Salon
Chardonnay only; good aged vintage; rich finesse

Taittinger
light, dry, complex, distinguished, elegant

De Venoge
reliable; well-made

Veuve Clicquot-Ponsardin
assertive, distinguished, mature

Glossary

L'assemblage – the blending of the wines

blanc de blancs – white wine made from white grapes alone

blanc de noirs – white wine made from black grapes

brut – Champagne with up to 15g of sugar per litre

Le chef de cave – the person in charge of cellar operations including the blending of the *cuvée*. A top position in any firm

Les coteaux champenois – the still wines from any Champagne region

Une crayère – a Roman chalk quarry used as a cellar

crémant – Champagne with about half the usual amount of *mousse*; also sparkling

Le cru – the growth of a quality grape, usually used to signify a specific vineyard

Une cuve – a vat

La cuvée – the blend

Le dégorgement – the disgorging of the first temporary cork

déguster – to taste wine

demi-sec – Champagne with 33–50g of sugar per litre

Le dosage (see *liqueur d'expédition*)

doux – Champagne with in excess of 50g of sugar per litre

L'échelle des crus – the percentage classification of the Champagne *crus*

extra-sec – Champagne with 12–20g of sugar per litre

Un grand cru – a fine growth; usually a reference to a top quality vineyard (see also *premier cru*)

Une Grande Marque – a famous Champagne brand

Les lattes – the lathes that separate the bottles while they are laid down on their sides to age

les lies – the lees

Le liqueur d'expédition – the mixture of sugar and wine added to bottled wine before it is finally sealed to adjust the degree of sweetness required by different Champagne markets

La marque – the brand

millésime – vintage year

mono-cru – wine from one vineyard growth

La mousse – the sparkle in Champagne

mousseux – sparkling

Un négociant – a shipper of wine

Un négociant-manipulant – a person (or a firm) that makes and markets Champagne

Un oenologue – a wine specialist, often with a university degree in the subject

Une pièce – a traditional measure of Champagne (205 litres)

Un premier cru – a vineyard that produces top quality grapes

Une presse – a press

La prise de mousse – the evolution of the bubbles in Champagne during fermentation

Une pupitre – the slotted board in which the bottles are placed to be riddled

Le rebêche – the juice that is extracted from grapes after the *deuxième taille*

Un récoltant-manipulant – a person who grows and makes Champagne

Le remuage – the riddling of the Champagne bottles which moves any dead yeast cells down to the cork where they can be removed.

Le remueur – the skilled worker who riddles the bottles

sec – Champagne with 17–23g of sugar per litre

Le sous-sol – the subsoil

Sur les pointes – bottles stacked upside down, cork to punt

tailler – to prune

Les tailles – the juice that is pressed from the grapes after the juice reserved for the *vin de cuve* has been collected. The *première tailles* are the first 410l (90gal) of juice; the *deuxième tailles* are the next 205l (45gal)

Les vendanges – the harvest of the grapes

Les vignerons – the vine workers, who sometimes own the vineyards they cultivate

vin de cuvée – the first 2000l (440gal) of juice from the pressing of the grapes

Bibliography

Allen, H. Warner *A History of Wine* Faber & Faber 1961

Arlott, John *Krug, House of Champagne* Davis-Poynter 1976

Asher, Gerald *On Wine* Jill Norman 1983

Barber, Noel *A Farewell to France* Hodder and Stoughton 1986

Bonal, François *La Livre d'Or du Champagne* Editions du Grand Pont, 1984

Booth, David *The Art of wine-making in all its branchs* London 1834

Brillat-Savarin *La Psychologie du goût* Paris 1826

Caraman Chimay, Princesse de *Madame Veuve Clicquot-Ponsardin. Sa vie, son temps* Reims 1956

Chaptal, Comte Jean Antoine *Traité Théorique sur la Culture de la Vigne* Paris 1859

Chesterfield, Lord *Lord Chesterfield's Witticisms or the Grand Pantheon of Genius, Sentiments and Taste* London 1772

CIVC (Epernay) *Cooking with Champagne* Lallemand 1970

Cooper, Sir Alfred Duff *Old Men Forget* Rupert Hart-Davis 1953

Crubellier, Maurice and Juillard, Charles *Histoire de la Champagne* Paris 1952

Custine, Marquis de *La Russie en 1839* Paris 1843

Dumay, Raymond *Guide du Vin* Stock 1967

Forbes, Patrick *Champagne. The wine, the land and the people* Victor Gollancz 1967

Gandon, Yves *Champagne* Neuchatel 1958

Guillemot, A. *Contes, légendes, veilles coutumes de la Marne* Châlons-sur-Marne 1908

Healy, Maurice *Stay me with Flagons* Michael Joseph 1940

Heidsieck, Marcel and Patrick *Vie de Charles Heidsieck* Reims 1962

Heron de Villefosse, Marie Henri Antoine René *Les Grandes Heures de la Champagne* Librairie Academique 1971

Hodez, Roger *La Protection des vins de Champagne par l'appellation d'origine* Paris 1952

Holland, Vyvyan *Drink and be Merry* Victor Gollancz 1967

Hollande, Maurice *Sur les routes de Champagne* Editions Michaud 1970

Hurault, Abbé *Saint Vincent, martyr, patron des vignerons* Châlons-sur-Marne 1910

Johnson, Hugh *Wine* Thomas Nelson 1966

Johnson, Hugh *World Atlas of Wine* Simon and Schuster 1971

Jubainville, Arbois de *Les Comtes de Champagne* Paris 1859

Larousse Gastronomique Paul Hamlyn 1961

Lichine, Alexis *Encyclopedia of Wines and Spirits* Cassell 1967

MacCuloch, John *Remarks on the art of making wine, with suggestions for the application of its principles to the improvement of domestic wines* London 1821

Magnin, Guy *Le Prestige de la bouteille de champagne depuis quatre siècles* Grenoble 1981

Maury, Dr. E.A. *Soignez-vous par le vin* Paris 1974

McDouall, Robin and Bush, Sheila *Recipes from a Château in Champagne* Victor Gollancz 1983

Medieval Academy of America *The Court of Champagne as a Literary Centre* Cambridge University Press, Massachusetts 1961

Odart, Comte *Manuel du vigneron* Paris 1861

Oliver, Raymond *The French at Table* Wine and Food Society 1967

Parisot, Magdaleine *Champagne, Ardennes* Librairie Hachette 1971

Price, Pamela Vandyke *Guide to the Wines of Champagne* Pitman 1984

Ray, Cyril *Bollinger* Peter Davies 1971

Ray, Cyril *The Wines of France* Allen Lane 1976

Saint-Evremond *Oeuvres de Monsieur de Saint-Evremond, avec la vie de l'auteur* Des Maizeaux, Amsterdam 1726

Salleron, J. *Etudes sur le vin mousseux* Paris 1886

Simon, André *Wines of the World* MacDonald 1967

Simon, André *The History of Champagne* Ebury Press 1962

Stevenson, Tom *Champagne* Sotheby's Publications 1986

Willow Books *Arlott on Wine* Collins 1986

Weinbold, Rudolf *Vivat Bacchus* Argus 1978

Vizetelly, Henry *A History of Champagne* London 1882

Vizetelly, Henry *Facts about champagne and other sparkling wines* London 1879

Vogüé, Comte Bertrand de *Madame Veuve Clicquot à la conquête pacifique de la Russie* Reims 1960

Index

Figures in *italic type* are illustration references.

Acknowledgements

The author would like to extend his special thanks to the following people:

Philippe le Tixerant, director of Information at the *Comité Interprofessionel du Vin de Champagne*; Axel de Réau, Directeur d'Acceuil of the CIVC; Jean Couten for his encouragement and the information about Hautvillers and Dom Pérignon; François Bonal for his advice and his marvellously complete *Livre d'Or du Champagne*; André Enders, director of the CIVC; Malcolm McIntyre, director of the Champagne Information Centre in London and his able staff, especially Kirsteen Hay; Pauline Hallam of the French Tourist Office in London; Joseph Dargent for his support and encouragement; Christian Bizot of Champagne Bollinger; Henri Geoffroy of the Co-opérative de l'Union Champagne; M. Hubert of Champagne Deutz & Geldermann; Gijsbert Hooft-Graafland of Champagne Charles Heidsieck; M. Delaître of Champagne Heidsieck & Cie. Monopole; François Louis Bernard of Champagne Jacquart; Henri and Rémi Krug, and Mme. Catherine Seydoux of Champagne Krug; Jean-Baptiste Lanson of Champagne Lanson; Emmanuel de la Giraudière of Champagne Laurent-Perrier; M. Augustin of Champagne Mercier; Yves Benard and Jean Paul Médard of Champagne Moët & Chandon; M. Cense of Champagne Mumm; Michel Budin of Champagne Perrier-Jouët; Fréderic Heidsieck of Piper-Heidsieck; Christian de Billy of Champagne Pol Roger; M. Derville of Champagne Pommery & Greno; Mme. Madeleine Roche of Champagne Louis Roederer; Mme. Michele Discrit of Champagne Ruinart; Mme. Marie-Josie Couvreur of Champagne Taittinger; Yvan Navacelle of Champagne Veuve Clicquot-Ponsardin; Patrick Forbes; Nancy Jarratt of Moët & Chandon in London; Mme. Nadine Heidsieck, a mine of information on Reims Cathedral; Marie Pierre Thierry of the CIVC; Bettina McNulty for her contributions, her unflagging support *and* her typing skills; and Emma Warlow for her admirable editorial advice and guidance.

The Paul Press would like to thank the following people and organizations to whom copyright in the photographs noted belongs;

10, 11 Jon Wyand; 14, 15 CIVC; 16 Jon Wyand; 17, 18 John Topham; 19 Mercier Champagne; 20 Pommery & Greno Champagne; 23 John Topham; 24, 25, 25(t), 27, 28 Mansell Collection; 30, 31, 31(t) Moët & Chandon (London); 32 Mansell Collection; 34, 35 Krug Champagne; 36 John Topham; 38, 39 Jon Wyand; 40 Moët & Chandon (London); 42, 43 Jon Wyand; 45, 47, 49 Mary Evans Picture Library; 50 John Freeman; 52, 53 Jon Wyand; 54, 55 CIVC; 56, 56(b), 57 H. Parrot & Co. (Veuve Clicquot-Ponsardin); 58(b) CIVC; 58, 59 60 Pommery & Greno Champagne; 61 CIVC; 63, 64, 65 Jon Wyand; 66 Pommery & Greno Champagne; 67(t) Mercier; 67(c) CIVC; 67(b) Heidsieck Champagne; 68, 69, 71 CIVC; 72 John Topham; 73 Pommery & Greno Champagne; 75 CIVC; 76, 77 H. Parrot & Co (Veuve Clicquot-Ponsardin); 77(t), 78 Moët & Chandon (London); 79 CIVC; 80, 81 Mansell Collection; 82, 83 Moët & Chandon (London); 84, 85 Bollinger Champagne; 88, 89 CIVC; 89 John Topham; 91, 92 Krug Champagne; 94 Laurent-Perrier Champagne; 97(t) Moët & Chandon (London); 97(b) Jon Wyand; 98, 99 Moët & Chandon (London); 100, 101, 101(t) Mercier Champagne; 103, 104, 105, 105(t) Mumm Champagne; 106 Mansell Collection; 108, 109 Heidsieck Champagne; 110, 111, 112, Pol Roger Champagne; 113 Pommery & Greno Champagne; 114 Mansell Collection; 117 Pommery & Greno Champagne; 118, 119 John Freeman; 124, 125 Moët & Chandon (London); 126 John Topham; 127(l) Moët & Chandon (London); 127(r) John Topham; 128, 129 Bollinger Champagne; 130 Anthony Blake; 137 Mary Evans Picture Library; 138 CIVC; 141 Moët & Chandon (London); 145 Jon Wyand; 147 Mary Evans Picture Library.